NECESSITY OF PRAYER

by

EM BOUNDS

BRITISH LIBRARY CATALOGUING IN PUBLICATION DATA
A RECORD OF THIS PUBLICATION IS AVAILABLE
FROM THE BRITISH LIBRARY

ISBN 978-1-84685-928-1

PUBLISHED 2008 BY
DIGGORY PRESS

DIGGORY PRESS LTD
THREE RIVERS, MINIONS, LISKEARD, CORNWALL, PL14 5LE, UK
DIGGORY PRESS, INC.,
GOODYEAR, ARIZONA, 85338, USA
WWW.DIGGORYPRESS.COM

NECESSITY OF PRAYER

I

PRAYER AND FAITH

"A dear friend of mine who was quite a lover of the chase, told me the following story: 'Rising early one morning,' he said, 'I heard the baying of a score of deerhounds in pursuit of their quarry. Looking away to a broad, open field in front of me, I saw a young fawn making its way across, and giving signs, moreover, that its race was well-nigh run. Reaching the rails of the enclosure, it leaped over and crouched within ten feet from where I stood. A moment later two of the hounds came over, when the fawn ran in my direction and pushed its head between my legs. I lifted the little thing to my breast, and, swinging round and round, fought off the dogs. I felt, just then, that all the dogs in the West could not, and should not capture that fawn after its weakness had appealed to my strength.' So is it, when human helplessness appeals to Almighty God. Well do I remember when the hounds of sin were after my soul, until, at last, I ran into the arms of Almighty God."

A. C. DIXON

IN any study of the principles, and procedure of prayer, of its activities and enterprises, first place, must, of necessity, be given to faith. It is the initial quality in the heart of any man who essays to talk to the Unseen. He must, out of sheer helplessness, stretch forth hands of faith. He *must* believe, where he cannot prove. In the ultimate issue, prayer is simply faith, claiming its natural yet marvellous prerogatives -- faith taking possession of its illimitable inheritance. True godliness is just as true, steady, and persevering in the realm of faith as it is in the province of prayer. Moreover: when faith ceases to pray, it ceases to live.

Faith does the impossible because it brings God to undertake for us, and nothing is impossible with God. How great -- without qualification or limitation -- is the power of faith! If doubt be banished from the heart, and unbelief made stranger there, what we ask of God shall surely come to pass, and a believer hath vouchsafed to him "whatsoever he saith."

Prayer projects faith on God, and God on the world. Only God can move mountains, but faith and prayer move God. In His cursing of the fig-tree our Lord demonstrated His power. Following that, He proceeded to declare, that large powers were committed to faith and prayer, not in order to kill but to make alive, not to blast but to bless.

At this point in our study, we turn to a saying of our Lord, which there is need to emphasize, since it is the very keystone of the arch of faith and prayer.

> *"Therefore I say unto you, What things soever ye desire when ye pray, believe that ye receive them, and ye shall have them."*

We should ponder well that statement -- "Believe that ye receive them, and ye shall have them." Here is described a faith which realizes, which appropriates, which *takes*. Such faith is a consciousness of the Divine, an experienced communion, a realized certainty.

Is faith growing or declining as the years go by? Does faith stand strong and four square, these days, as iniquity abounds and the love of many grows cold? Does faith maintain its hold, as religion tends to become a mere formality and worldliness increasingly prevails? The enquiry of our Lord, may, with great appropriateness, be ours. "When the Son of Man cometh," He asks, "shall He find faith on the earth?" We believe that He will, and it is ours, in this our day, to see to it that the lamp of faith is trimmed and burning, lest He come who *shall* come, and that right early.

Faith is the foundation of Christian character and the security of the soul. When Jesus was looking forward to Peter's denial, and cautioning him against it, He said unto His disciple:

> *"Simon, Simon, behold, Satan hath desired to have you, to sift you as wheat; but I have prayed for thee, that thy faith fall not."*

Our Lord was declaring a central truth; it was Peter's faith He was seeking to guard; for well He knew that when faith is broken down, the foundations of spiritual life give way, and the entire structure of religious experience falls. It was Peter's faith which needed guarding. Hence Christ's solicitude for the welfare of His disciple's soul and His determination to fortify Peter's faith by His own all-prevailing prayer.

In his *Second Epistle*, Peter has this idea in mind when speaking of growth in grace as a measure of safety in the Christian life, and as implying fruitfulness.

> *"And besides this,"* he declares, *"giving diligence, add to your faith virtue; and to virtue knowledge; and to knowledge temperance; and to temperance patience; and to patience godliness."*

Of this additioning process, faith was the starting-point -- the basis of the other graces of the Spirit. Faith was the foundation on which other things were to be built. Peter does not enjoin his readers to add to works or gifts or virtues but to *faith*. Much depends on starting right in this business of growing in grace. There is a Divine order, of which Peter was aware; and so he goes on to declare that we are to give diligence to making our calling and election sure, which election is rendered certain adding to faith which, in turn, is done by constant, earnest praying. Thus faith is kept alive by prayer, and every step taken, in this adding of grace to grace, is accompanied by prayer.

The faith which pcreates powerful praying is the faith which centres itself on a powerful Person. Faith in Christ's ability to *do* and to *do greatly*, is the faith which prays greatly. Thus the leper lay hold upon the power of Christ. "Lord, if Thou wilt," he cried, "Thou canst make me clean." In this instance, we are shown how faith centered in Christ's ability to *do*, and how it secured the healing power.

It was concerning this very point, that Jesus questioned the blind men who came to Him for healing:

> *"Believe ye that I am able to do this?"*
> *He asks. "They said unto Him, Yea,*
> *Lord. Then touched He their eyes,*
> *saying, According to your faith be it*
> *unto you."*

It was to inspire faith in His ability to *do* that Jesus left behind Him, that last, great statement, which, in the final analysis, is a ringing challenge to faith. "All power," He declared, "is given unto Me in heaven and in earth."

Again: faith is obedient; it goes when commanded, as did the nobleman, who came to Jesus, in the day of His flesh, and whose son was grievously sick.

Moreover: such faith acts. Like the man who was born blind, it goes to wash in the pool of Siloam when *told* to wash. Like Peter on Gennesaret it casts the net where Jesus commands, instantly, without question or doubt. Such faith takes away the stone from the grave of Lazarus promptly. A praying faith keeps the commandments of God and does those things which are well pleasing in His sight. It asks, "Lord, what wilt Thou have me to do?" and answers quickly, "Speak, Lord, Thy servant heareth." Obedience helps faith, and faith, in turn, helps obedience. To do God's will is essential to true faith, and faith is necessary to implicit obedience.

Yet faith is called upon, and that right often to wait in patience before God, and is prepared for God's seeming delays in answering prayer. Faith does not grow disheartened because prayer is not immediately honoured; it takes God at His Word, and lets Him take what time He chooses in fulfilling His purposes, and in carrying on His work. There is bound to be much delay and long days of waiting for true faith, but faith accepts the conditions -- knows there will be delays in answering prayer, and regards such delays as times of testing, in the which, it is privileged to show its mettle, and the stern stuff of which it is made.

The case of Lazarus was an instance of where there was delay, where the faith of two good women was sorely tried: Lazarus was critically ill, and his sisters sent for Jesus. But, without any known reason, our Lord delayed His going to the relief of His sick friend. The plea was urgent and touching -- "Lord, behold, he whom Thou lovest is sick," -- but the Master is not moved by it, and the women's earnest request seemed to fall on deaf ears. What a trial to faith! Furthermore: our Lord's tardiness appeared to bring about hopeless disaster. While Jesus tarried, Lazarus died.

But the delay of Jesus was exercised in the interests of a greater good. Finally, He makes His way to the home in Bethany.

> *"Then said Jesus unto them plainly, Lazarus is dead. And I am glad for your sakes, that I was not there, to the intent ye may believe; nevertheless let us go unto him."*

Fear not, O tempted and tried believer, Jesus *will* come, if patience be exercised, and faith hold fast. His delay will serve to make His coming the more richly blessed. Pray on. Wait on. Thou canst not fail. If Christ delay, wait for Him. In His own good time, He *will* come, and will not tarry.

Delay is often the test and the strength of faith. How much patience is required when these times of testing come! Yet faith gathers strength by waiting and praying. Patience has its perfect work in the school of delay. In some instances, delay is of the very essence of the prayer. God has to do many things, antecedent to giving the final answer -- things which are essential to the lasting good of him who is requesting favour at His hands.

Jacob prayed, with point and ardour, to be delivered from Esau. But before that prayer could be answered, there was much to be done with, and for Jacob. He must be changed, as well as Esau. Jacob had to be made into a new man, before Esau could be. Jacob had to be converted to God, before Esau could be converted to Jacob.

Among the large and luminous utterances of Jesus concerning prayer, none is more arresting than this:

> *"Verily, verily, I say unto you, He that believeth on Me, the works that I do shall he do also; and greater works than these shall he do; because I go unto My Father. And whatsoever ye shall ask in My Name, that will I do, that the Father may be glorified in the Son. If ye shall ask anything in My Name, I will do it."*

How wonderful are these statements of what God will do in answer to prayer! Of how great importance these ringing words, prefaced, as they are, with the most solemn verity! Faith in Christ is the basis of all working, and of all praying. All wonderful works depend on wonderful praying, and all praying is done in the Name of Jesus Christ. Amazing lesson, of wondrous simplicity, is this praying in the name of the Lord Jesus! All other conditions are depreciated, everything else is renounced, save Jesus only. The name of Christ -- the Person of our Lord and Saviour Jesus Christ -- must be supremely sovereign, in the hour and article of prayer.

If Jesus dwell at the fountain of my life; if the currents of His life have displaced and superseded all self-currents; if implicit obedience to Him be the inspiration and force of every movement of my life, then He can safely commit the praying to my will, and pledge Himself, by an obligation as profound as His own nature, that whatsoever is asked shall be granted. Nothing can be clearer, more distinct, more unlimited both in application and extent, than the exhortation and urgency of Christ, "Have faith in God."

Faith covers temporal as well as spiritual needs. Faith dispels all undue anxiety and needless care about what shall be eaten, what shall he drunk, what shall be worn. Faith lives in the present, and regards the day as being sufficient unto the evil thereof. It lives day by day, and dispels all fears for the morrow. Faith brings great ease of mind and perfect peace of heart.

> *"Thou wilt keep him in perfect peace whose mind is stayed on Thee: because he trusted in Thee."*

When we pray, "Give us this day our daily bread," we are, in a measure, shutting tomorrow out of our prayer. We do not live in tomorrow but in today. We do not seek tomorrow's grace or tomorrow's bread. They thrive best, and get most out of life, who live in the living present. They pray best who pray for today's needs, not for tomorrow's, which may render our prayers unnecessary and redundant by not existing at all!

True prayers are born of present trials and present needs. Bread, for today, is bread enough. Bread given for today is the strongest sort of pledge that there will be bread tomorrow. Victory today, is the assurance of victory tomorrow. Our prayers need to be focussed upon the present, We must trust God today, and leave the morrow entirely with Him. The present is ours; the future belongs to God. Prayer is the task and duty of each recurring day -- daily prayer for daily needs.

As every day demands its bread, so every day demands its prayer. No amount of praying, done today, will suffice for tomorrow's praying. On the other hand, no praying for tomorrow is of any great value to us today. To-day's manna is what we need; tomorrow God will see that our needs are supplied. This is the faith which God seeks to inspire. So leave tomorrow, with its cares, its needs, its troubles, in God's hands. There is no storing tomorrow's grace or tomorrow's praying; neither is there any laying-up of today's grace, to meet tomorrow's necessities. We cannot have tomorrow's grace, we cannot eat tomorrow's bread, we cannot do tomorrow's praying. "Sufficient unto the day is the evil thereof;" and, most assuredly, if we possess faith, sufficient also, will be the good.

II

PRAYER AND FAITH (Continued)

"The guests at a certain hotel were being rendered uncomfortable by repeated strumming on a piano, done by a little girl who possessed no knowledge of music. They complained to the proprietor with a view to having the annoyance stopped. 'I am sorry you are annoyed,' he said. 'But the girl is the child of one of my very best guests. I can scarcely ask her not to touch the piano. But her father, who is away for a day or so, will return tomorrow. You can then approach him, and have the matter set right.' When the father returned, he found his daughter in the reception-room and, as usual, thumping on the piano. He walked up behind the child and, putting his arms over her shoulders, took her hands in his, and produced some most beautiful music. Thus it may be with us, and thus it will be, some coming day. Just now, we can produce little but clamour and disharmony; but, one day, the Lord Jesus will take hold of our hands of faith and prayer, and use them to bring forth the music of the skies."

ANON

GENUINE, authentic faith must be definite and free of doubt. Not simply general in character; not a mere belief in the being, goodness and power of God, but a faith which believes that the things which "he saith, shall come to pass." As the faith is specific, so the answer likewise will be definite: "He shall have whatsoever he saith." Faith and prayer select the things, and God commits Himself to do the very things which faith and persevering prayer nominate, and petition Him to accomplish.

The American Revised Version renders the twenty-fourth verse of the eleventh chapter of Mark, thus: "Therefore I say unto you, All things whatsoever ye pray and ask for, believe that ye receive them, and ye shall have them." Perfect faith has always in its keeping what perfect prayer asks for. How large and unqualified is the area of operation -- the "All things whatsoever!" How definite and specific the promise -- "Ye shall have them!"

Our chief concern is with our faith, -- the problems of its growth, and the activities of its vigorous maturity. A faith which grasps and holds in its keeping the very things it asks for, without wavering, doubt or fear -- that is the faith we need -- faith, such as is a pearl of great price, in the process and practise of prayer.

The statement of our Lord about faith and prayer quoted above is of supreme importance. Faith must be definite, specific; an unqualified, unmistakable request for the things asked for. It is not to be a vague, indefinite, shadowy thing; it must be something more than an abstract belief in God's willingness and ability to do for us. It is to be a definite, specific, asking for, and expecting the things for which we ask. Note the reading of Mark 11:23:

> *"And shall not doubt in his heart, but*
> *shall believe that those things which he*
> *saith shall come to pass; he shall have*
> *whatever he saith."*

Just so far as the faith and the asking is definite, so also will the answer be. The giving is not to be something other than the things prayed for, but the actual things sought and named. "He shall have whatsoever he saith." It is all imperative, "He shall have." The granting is to be unlimited, both in quality and in quantity.

Faith and prayer select the subjects for petition, thereby determining what God is to do. "He shall have whatsoever he saith." Christ holds Himself ready to supply exactly, and fully, all the demands of faith and prayer. If the order on God be made clear, specific and definite, God will fill it, exactly in accordance with the presented terms.

Faith is not an abstract belief in the Word of God, nor a mere mental credence, nor a simple assent of the understanding and will; nor is it a passive acceptance of facts, however sacred or thorough. Faith is an operation of God, a Divine illumination, a holy energy implanted by the Word of God and the Spirit in the human soul -- a spiritual, Divine principle which takes of the Supernatural and makes it a thing apprehendable by the faculties of time and sense.

Faith deals with God, and is conscious of God. It deals with the Lord Jesus Christ and sees in Him a Saviour; it deals with God's Word, and lays hold of the truth; it deals with the Spirit of God, and is energized and inspired by its holy fire. God is the great objective of faith; for faith rests its whole weight on His Word. Faith is not an aimless act of the soul, but a looking to God and a resting upon His promises. Just as love and hope have always an objective so, also, has faith. Faith is not believing just *anything*; it is believing God, resting in Him, trusting His Word.

Faith gives birth to prayer, and grows stronger, strikes deeper, rises higher, in the struggles and wrestlings of mighty petitioning. Faith is the substance of things hoped for, the assurance and realization of the inheritance of the saints. Faith, too, is humble and persevering. It can wait and pray; it can stay on its knees, or lie in the dust. It is the one great condition of prayer; the lack of it lies at the root of all poor praying, feeble praying, little praying, unanswered praying.

The nature and meaning of faith is more demonstrable in what it does, than it is by reason of any definition given it. Thus, if we turn to the record of faith given us in that great honour roll, which constitutes the eleventh chapter of Hebrews, we see something of the wonderful results of faith. What a glorious list it is -- that of these men and women of faith! What marvellous achievements are there recorded, and set to the credit of faith! The inspired writer, exhausting his resources in cataloguing the Old Testament saints, who were such notable examples of wonderful faith, finally exclaims:

> *"And what shall I more say? For the time would fail me to tell of Gideon and*

Barak, and of Samson, and of Jephthae;
of David also, and Samuel, and of the
prophets."

And then the writer of *Hebrews* goes on again, in a wonderful strain, telling of the unrecorded exploits wrought through the faith of the men of old, "of whom the world was not worthy." "All these," he says, "obtained a good report through faith."

What an era of glorious achievements would dawn for the Church and the world, if only there could be reproduced a race of saints of like mighty faith, of like wonderful praying! It is not the intellectually great that the Church needs; nor is it men of wealth that the times demand. It is not people of great social influence that this day requires. Above everybody and everything else, it is men of faith, men of mighty prayer, men and women after the fashion of the saints and heroes enumerated in *Hebrews*, who "obtained a good report through faith," that the Church and the whole wide world of humanity needs.

Many men, of this day, obtain a good report because of their money-giving, their great mental gifts and talents, but few there be who obtain a "good report" because of their great faith in God, or because of the wonderful things which are being wrought through their great praying. Today, as much as at any time, we need men of great faith and men who are great in prayer. These are the two cardinal virtues which make men great in the eyes of God, the two things which create conditions of real spiritual success in the life and work of the Church. It is our chief concern to see that we maintain a faith of such quality and texture, as counts before God; which grasps, and holds in its keeping, the things for which it asks, without doubt and without fear.

Doubt and fear are the twin foes of faith. Sometimes, they actually usurp the place of faith, and although we pray, it is a restless, disquieted prayer that we offer, uneasy and often complaining. Peter failed to walk on Gennesaret because he permitted the waves to break over him and swamp the power of his faith. Taking his eyes from the Lord and regarding the water all about him, he began to sink and had to cry for succour -- "Lord, save, or I perish!"

Doubts should never be cherished, nor fears harboured. Let none cherish the delusion that he is a martyr to fear and doubt. It is no credit to any man's mental capacity to cherish doubt of God, and no comfort can possibly derive from such a thought. Our eyes should be taken off self, removed from our own weakness and allowed to rest implicitly upon God's strength. "Cast not away therefore your confidence, which hath great recompence of reward." A simple, confiding faith, living day by day, and casting its burden on the Lord, each hour of the day, will dissipate fear, drive away misgiving and deliver from doubt:

> *"Be careful for nothing, but in everything, by supplication and prayer, with thanksgiving, let your requests be made known unto God."*

That is the Divine cure for all fear, anxiety, and undue concern of soul, all of which are closely akin to doubt and unbelief. This is the Divine prescription for securing the peace which passeth all understanding, and keeps the heart and mind in quietness and peace.

All of us need to mark well and heed the caution given in *Hebrews:* "Take heed, brethren, lest there be in any of you an evil heart of unbelief, in departing from the living God."

We need, also, to guard against unbelief as we would against an enemy. Faith needs to be cultivated. We need to keep on praying, "Lord, increase our faith," for faith is susceptible of increase. Paul's tribute to the Thessalonians was, that their faith grew exceedingly. Faith is increased by exercise, by being put into use. It is nourished by sore trials.

> *"That the trial of your faith, being much more precious than of gold that perisheth, though it be tried with fire, might be found unto praise and honour*

*and glow at the appearing of Jesus
Christ."*

Faith grows by reading and meditating upon the Word of God. Most, and best of all, faith thrives in an atmosphere of prayer.

It would be well, if all of us were to stop, and inquire personally of ourselves: "Have I faith in God? Have I *real* faith, -- faith which keeps me in perfect peace, about the things of earth and the things of heaven?" This is the most important question a man can propound and expect to be answered. And there is another question, closely akin to it in significance and importance -- "Do I really pray to God so that He hears me and answers my prayers? And do I truly pray unto God so that I get direct from God the things I ask of Him?"

It was claimed for Augustus Caesar that he found Rome a city of wood, and left it a city of marble. The pastor who succeeds in changing his people from a prayerless to a prayerful people, has done a greater work than did Augustus in changing a city from wood to marble. And after all, this is the prime work of the preacher. Primarily, he is dealing with prayerless people -- with people of whom it is said, "God is not in all their thoughts." Such people he meets everywhere, and all the time. His main business is to turn them from being forgetful of God, from being devoid of faith, from being prayerless, so that they become people who habitually pray, who believe in God, remember Him and do His will. The preacher is not sent to merely induce men to join the Church, nor merely to get them to do better. It is to get them to pray, to trust God, and to keep God ever before their eyes, that they may not sin against Him.

The work of the ministry is to change unbelieving sinners into praying and believing saints. The call goes forth by Divine authority, "Believe on the Lord Jesus Christ, and thou shalt be saved." We catch a glimpse of the tremendous importance of faith and of the great value God has set upon it, when we remember that He has made it the one indispensable condition of being saved. "By grace are ye saved, through faith." Thus, when we contemplate the great importance of prayer, we find faith standing immediately by its side. By faith are we saved, and by faith we *stay* saved. Prayer introduces us to a life of faith. Paul declared that the life he lived, he lived by faith in the Son of God, who loved him and gave Himself for him -- that he walked by faith and not by sight.

Prayer is absolutely dependent upon faith. Virtually, it has no existence apart from it, and accomplishes nothing unless it be its inseparable companion. Faith makes prayer effectual, and in a certain important sense, must precede it.

> *"For he that cometh to God must believe*
> *that He is, and that He is a rewarder of*
> *them that diligently seek Him."*

Before prayer ever starts toward God; before its petition is preferred, before its requests are made known -- faith must have gone on ahead; must have asserted its belief in the existence of God; must have given its assent to the gracious truth that "God is a rewarder of those that diligently seek His face." This is the primary step in praying. In this regard, while faith does not bring the blessing, yet it puts prayer in a position to ask for it, and leads to another step toward realization, by aiding the petitioner to believe that God is able and willing to bless.

Faith starts prayer to work -- clears the way to the mercy-seat. It gives assurance, first of all, that there is a mercy-seat, and that there the High Priest awaits the pray-ers and the prayers. Faith opens the way for prayer to approach God. But it does more. It accompanies prayer at every step she takes. It is her inseparable companion and when requests are made unto God, it is faith which turns the asking into obtaining. And faith follows prayer, since the spiritual life into which a believer is led by prayer, is a life of faith. The one prominent characteristic of the experience into which believers are brought through prayer, is not a life of works, but of faith.

Faith makes prayer strong, and gives it patience to wait on God. Faith believes that God is a rewarder. No truth is more clearly revealed in the Scriptures than this, while none is more encouraging. Even the closet has its promised reward, "He that seeth in secret, shall reward thee openly," while the most insignificant service rendered to a disciple in the name of the Lord, surely receives its reward. And to this precious truth faith gives its hearty assent.

Yet faith is narrowed down to one particular thing -- it does not believe that God will reward everybody, nor that He is a rewarder of all who pray, but that He is a rewarder of them that *diligently seek Him*. Faith rests its care on diligence in prayer, and gives assurance and encouragement to diligent seekers after God, for it is they, alone, who are richly rewarded when they pray.

We need constantly to be reminded that faith is the one inseparable condition of successful praying. There are other considerations entering into the exercise, but faith is the final, the one indispensable condition of true praying. As it is written in a familiar, primary declaration: "Without faith, it is impossible to please Him."

James puts this truth very plainly.

> *"If any of you lack wisdom," he says, "let him ask of God, that giveth to all men liberally, and upbraideth not, and it shall be given him. But let him ask in faith, nothing wavering. For he that wavereth (or doubteth) is like a wave of the sea, driven with the wind and tossed. For let not that man think that he shall receive any thing of the Lord."*

Doubting is always put under the ban, because it stands as a foe to faith and hinders effectual praying. In the First Epistle to Timothy Paul gives us an invaluable truth relative to the conditions of successful praying, which he thus lays down: "I will therefore that men pray everywhere, lifting up holy hands, without wrath and doubting."

All questioning must be watched against and eschewed. Fear and peradventure have no place in true praying. Faith must assert itself and bid these foes to prayer depart.

Too much authority cannot be attributed to faith; but prayer is the sceptre by which it signalizes its power. How much of spiritual wisdom there is in the following advice written by an eminent old divine.

> *"Would you be freed from the bondage to corruption?"* he asks. *"Would you grow in grace in general and grow in grace in particular? If you would, your way is plain. Ask of God more faith. Beg of Him morning, and noon and night, while you walk by the way, while you sit in the house, when you lie down and when you rise up; beg of Him simply to impress Divine things more deeply on your heart, to give you more and more of the substance of things hoped for and of the evidence of things not seen."*

Great incentives to pray are furnished in Holy Scriptures, and our Lord closes His teaching about prayer, with the assurance and promise of heaven. The presence of Jesus Christ in heaven, the preparation for His saints which He is making there, and the assurance that He will come again to receive them -- how all this helps the weariness of praying, strengthens its conflicts, sweetens its arduous toil! These things are the star of hope to prayer, the wiping away of its tears, the putting of the odour of heaven into the bitterness of its cry. The spirit of a pilgrim greatly facilitates praying. An earth-bound, earth-satisfied spirit cannot pray. In such a heart, the flame of spiritual desire is either gone out or smouldering in faintest glow. The wings of its faith are clipped, its eyes are filmed, its tongue silenced. But they, who in unswerving faith and unceasing prayer, wait continually upon the Lord, *do* renew their strength, *do* mount up with wings as eagles, *do* run, and are not weary, *do* walk, and not faint.

III

PRAYER AND TRUST

"One evening I left my office in New York, with a bitterly cold wind in my face. I had with me, (as I thought) my thick, warm muffler, but when I proceeded to button-up against the storm, I found that it was gone. I turned back, looked along the streets, searched my office, but in vain. I realized, then, that I must have dropped it, and prayed God that I might find it; for such was the state of the weather, that it would be running a great risk to proceed without it. I looked, again, up and down the surrounding streets, but without success. Suddenly, I saw a man on the opposite side of the road holding out something in his hand. I crossed over and asked him if that were my muffler? He handed it to me saying, 'It was blown to me by the wind.' He who rides upon the storm, had used the wind as a means of answering prayer."

WILLIAM HORST.

PRAYER does not stand alone. It is not an isolated duty and independent principle. It lives in association with other Christian duties, is wedded to other principles, is a partner with other graces. But to faith, prayer is indissolubly joined. Faith gives it colour and tone, shapes its character, and secures its results.

Trust is faith become absolute, ratified, consummated. There is, when all is said and done, a sort of venture in faith and its exercise. But trust *is firm belief*, it is faith in full flower. Trust is a conscious act, a fact of which we are sensible. According to the Scriptural concept it is the eye of the new-born soul, and the ear of the renewed soul. It is the feeling of the soul, the spiritual eye, the ear, the taste, the feeling -- these one and all have to do with trust. How luminous, how distinct, how conscious, how powerful, and more than all, how Scriptural is such a trust! How different from many forms of modern belief, so feeble, dry, and cold! These new phases of belief bring no consciousness of their presence, no "Joy unspeakable and full of glory" results from their exercise. They are, for the most part, adventures in the peradventures of the soul. There is no safe, sure trust in anything. The whole transaction takes place in the realm of Maybe and Perhaps.

Trust like life, is feeling, though much more than feeling. An unfelt life is a contradiction; an unfelt trust is a misnomer, a delusion, a contradiction. Trust is the most felt of all attributes. It is *all* feeling, and it works only by love. An unfelt love is as impossible as an unfelt trust. The trust of which we are now speaking is a conviction. An unfelt conviction? How absurd!

Trust sees God doing things here and now. Yea, more. It rises to a lofty eminence, and looking into the invisible and the eternal, realizes that God has done things, and regards them as being already done. Trust brings eternity into the annals and happenings of time, transmutes the substance of hope into the reality of fruition, and changes promise into present possession. We know when we trust just as we know when we see, just as we are conscious of our sense of touch. Trust sees, receives, holds. Trust is its own witness.

Yet, quite often, faith is too weak to obtain God's greatest good, immediately; so it has to wait in loving, strong, prayerful, pressing obedience, until it grows in strength, and is able to bring down the eternal, into the realms of experience and time.

To this point, trust masses all its forces. Here it holds. And in the struggle, trust's grasp becomes mightier, and grasps, for itself, all that God has done for it in His eternal wisdom and plenitude of grace.

In the matter of waiting in prayer, mightiest prayer, faith rises to its highest plane and becomes indeed the gift of God. It becomes the blessed disposition and expression of the soul which is secured by a constant intercourse with, and unwearied application to God.

Jesus Christ clearly taught that faith was the condition on which prayer was answered. When our Lord had cursed the fig-tree, the disciples were much surprised that its withering had actually taken place, and their remarks indicated their in credulity. It was then that Jesus said to them, "Have faith in God."

> *"For verily I say unto you, That whosoever shall say unto this mountain, Be thou removed and be thou cast into the sea, and shall not doubt in his heart, but shall believe that those things which he saith shall come to pass, he shall have whatsoever he saith. Therefore, I say unto you, What things soever ye desire, when ye pray, believe that ye receive them, and ye shall have them."*

Trust grows nowhere so readily and richly as in the prayer-chamber. Its unfolding and development are rapid and wholesome when they are regularly and well kept. When these engagements are hearty and full and free, trust flourishes exceedingly. The eye and presence of God give vigorous life to trust, just as the eye and the presence of the sun make fruit and flower to grow, and all things glad and bright with fuller life.

"Have faith in God," "Trust in the Lord" form the keynote and foundation of prayer. Primarily, it is not trust in the Word of God, but rather trust in the Person of God. For trust in the Person of God must precede trust in the Word of God. "Ye believe in God, believe also in Me," is the demand our Lord makes on the personal trust of His disciples. The person of Jesus Christ must be central, to the eye of trust. This great truth Jesus sought to impress upon Martha, when her brother lay dead, in the home at Bethany. Martha asserted her belief in the fact of the resurrection of her brother:

> *"Martha saith unto Him, I know that he shall rise again in the resurrection at the last day."*

Jesus lifts her trust clear above the mere fact of the resurrection, to His own Person, by saying:

*"I am the resurrection and the life: he
that believeth in Me, though he were
dead, yet shall he live: and whosoever
liveth and believeth in Me, shall never
die. Believest thou this? She saith unto
Him, Yea, Lord: I believe that Thou art
the Christ, the Son of God, which should
come into the world."*

Trust, in an historical fact or in a mere record may be a very passive thing, but trust in a person vitalizes the quality, fructifies it, informs it with love. The trust which informs prayer centres in a Person.

Trust goes even further than this. The trust which inspires our prayer must be not only trust in the Person of God, and of Christ, but in their ability and willingness to grant the thing prayed for. It is not only, "Trust, ye, in the Lord," but, also, "for in the Lord Jehovah, is everlasting strength."

The trust which our Lord taught as a condition of effectual prayer, is not of the head but of the heart. It is trust which "doubteth not in his heart." Such trust has the Divine assurance that it shall be honoured with large and satisfying answers. The strong promise of our Lord brings faith down to the present, and counts on a present answer.

Do we believe, without a doubt? When we pray, do we believe, not that we shall receive the things for which we ask on a future day, but that we receive them, then and there? Such is the teaching of this inspiring Scripture. How we need to pray, "Lord, increase our faith," until doubt be gone, and implicit trust claims the promised blessings, as its very own.

This is no easy condition. It is reached only after many a failure, after much praying, after many waitings, after much trial of faith. May our faith so increase until we realize and receive all the fulness there is in that Name which guarantees to do so much.

Our Lord puts trust as the very foundation of praying. The background of prayer is trust. The whole issuance of Christ's ministry and work was dependent on implicit trust in His Father.

The centre of trust is God. Mountains of difficulties, and all other hindrances to prayer are moved out of the way by trust and his virile henchman, faith. When trust is perfect and without doubt, prayer is simply the outstretched hand, ready to receive. Trust perfected, is prayer perfected. Trust looks to receive the thing asked for -- and gets it. Trust is not a belief that God *can* bless, that He *will* bless, but that He *does* bless, here and now. Trust always operates in the present tense. Hope looks toward the future. Trust looks to the present. Hope expects. Trust possesses. Trust receives what prayer acquires. So that what prayer needs, at all times, is abiding and abundant trust.

Their lamentable lack of trust and resultant failure of the disciples to do what they were sent out to do, is seen in the case of the lunatic son, who was brought by his father to nine of them while their Master was on the Mount of Transfiguration. A boy, sadly afflicted, was brought to these men to be cured of his malady. They had been commissioned to do this very kind of work. This was a part of their mission. They attempted to cast out the devil from the boy, but had signally failed. The devil was too much for them. They were humiliated at their failure, and filled with shame, while their enemies were in triumph. Amid the confusion incident to failure Jesus draws near. He is informed of the circumstances, and told of the conditions connected therewith. Here is the succeeding account:

"Then Jesus answered and said, O faithless and perverse generation, how long shall I be with you? How long shall I suffer you? Bring him hither to me. And Jesus rebuked the devil, and he departed out of him and the child was cured from that very hour. And when He was come into the house, His disciples asked Him privately, Why could not we cast him out? And He said unto them, This kind can come forth by nothing but by prayer and fasting."

Wherein lay the difficulty with these men? They had been lax in cultivating their faith by prayer and, as a consequence, their trust utterly failed. They trusted not God, nor Christ, nor the authenticity of His mission, or their own. So has it been many a time since, in many a crisis in the Church of God. Failure has resulted from a lack of trust, or from a weakness of faith, and this, in turn, from a lack of prayerfulness. Many a failure in revival efforts has been traceable to the same cause. Faith had not been nurtured and made powerful by prayer. Neglect of the inner chamber is the solution of most spiritual failure. And this is as true of our personal struggles with the devil as was the case when we went forth to attempt to cast *out* devils. To be much on our knees in private communion with God is the only surety that we shall have Him with us either in our personal struggles, or in our efforts to convert sinners.

Everywhere, in the approaches of the people to Him, our Lord put trust in Him, and the divinity of His mission, in the forefront. He gave no definition of trust, and He furnishes no theological discussion of, or analysis of it; for He knew that men would see what faith was by what faith *did*; and from its free exercise trust grew up, spontaneously, in His presence. It was the product of His work, His power and His Person. These furnished and created an atmosphere most favourable for its exercise and development. Trust is altogether too splendidly simple for verbal definition; too hearty and spontaneous for theological terminology. The very simplicity of trust is that which staggers many people. They look away for some great thing to come to pass, while all the time "the word is nigh thee, even in thy mouth, and in thy heart."

When the saddening news of his daughter's death was brought to Jairus our Lord interposed: "Be not afraid," He said calmly, "only believe." To the woman with the issue of blood, who stood tremblingly before Him, He said:

> "Daughter, thy faith hath made thee
> whole; go in peace, and be whole of thy
> plague."

As the two blind men followed Him, pressing their way into the house, He said:

> *"According to your faith be it unto you.*
> *And their eyes were opened."*

When the paralytic was let down through the roof of the house, where Jesus was teaching, and placed before Him by four of his friends, it is recorded after this fashion:

> *"And Jesus seeing their faith, said unto*
> *the sick of the palsy: Son, be of good*
> *cheer; thy sins be forgiven thee."*

When Jesus dismissed the centurion whose servant was seriously ill, and who had come to Jesus with the prayer that He speak the healing word, without even going to his house, He did it in the manner following:

> *"And Jesus said unto the centurion, Go*
> *thy way; and as thou hast believed, so be*
> *it done unto thee. And his servant was*
> *healed in the selfsame hour."*

When the poor leper fell at the feet of Jesus and cried out for relief, "Lord, if Thou wilt, Thou canst make me clean," Jesus immediately granted his request, and the man glorified Him with a loud voice. Then Jesus said unto him, "Arise, go thy way; thy faith hath made thee whole."

The Syrophenician woman came to Jesus with the case of her afflicted daughter, making the case her own, with the prayer, "Lord, help me," making a fearful and heroic struggle. Jesus honours her faith and prayer, saying:

> *"O woman, great is thy faith: be it unto*
> *thee even as thou wilt. And her*
> *daughter was made whole from that*
> *very hour."*

After the disciples had utterly failed to cast the devil out of the epileptic boy, the father of the stricken lad came to Jesus with the plaintive and almost despairing cry, "If Thou canst do anything, have compassion on us and help us." But Jesus replied, "If thou canst believe, all things are possible to him that believeth."

Blind Bartimaeus sitting by the wayside, hears our Lord as He passes by, and cries out pitifully and almost despairingly, "Jesus, Thou son of David, have mercy on me." The keen ears of our Lord immediately catch the sound of prayer, and He says to the beggar:

> *"Go thy way; thy faith hath made thee*
> *whole. And immediately he received his*
> *sight, and followed Jesus in the way."*

To the weeping, penitent woman, washing His feet with her tears and wiping them with the hair of her head, Jesus speaks cheering, soul-comforting words: "Thy faith hath saved thee; go in peace."

One day Jesus healed ten lepers at one time, in answer to their united prayer, "Jesus, Master, have mercy on us," and He told them to go and show themselves to the priests. "And it came to pass as they went, they were cleansed."

IV

PRAYER AND DESIRE

"There are those who will mock me, and tell me to stick to my trade as a cobbler, and not trouble my mind with philosophy and theology. But the truth of God did so burn in my bones, that I took my pen in hand and began to set down what I had seen."

JACOB BEHMEN

DESIRE is not merely a simple wish; it is a deep seated craving; an intense longing, for attainment. In the realm of spiritual affairs, it is an important adjunct to prayer. So important is it, that one might say, almost, that desire is an absolute essential of prayer. Desire precedes prayer, accompanies it, is followed by it. Desire goes before prayer, and by it, created and intensified. Prayer is the oral expression of desire. If prayer is asking God for something, then prayer must be expressed. Prayer comes out into the open. Desire is silent. Prayer is heard; desire, unheard. The deeper the desire, the stronger the prayer. Without desire, prayer is a meaningless mumble of words. Such perfunctory, formal praying, with no heart, no feeling, no real desire accompanying it, is to be shunned like a pestilence. Its exercise is a waste of precious time, and from it, no real blessing accrues.

And yet even if it be discovered that desire is *honestly* absent, we should pray, anyway. We *ought* to pray. The "ought" comes in, in order that both desire and expression be cultivated. God's Word commands it. Our judgment tells us we ought to pray -- to pray whether we feel like it or not -- and not to allow our feelings to determine our habits of prayer. In such circumstance, we ought to pray for the *desire* to pray; for such a desire is God-given and heaven-born. We should pray for desire; then, when desire has been given, we should pray according to its dictates. Lack of spiritual desire should grieve us, and lead us to lament its absence, to seek earnestly for its bestowal, so that our praying, henceforth, should be an expression of "the soul's sincere desire."

A sense of need creates or should create, earnest desire. The stronger the sense of need, before God, the greater should be the desire, the more earnest the praying. The "poor in spirit" are eminently competent to pray.

Hunger is an active sense of physical need. It prompts the request for bread. In like manner, the inward consciousness of spiritual need creates desire, and desire breaks forth in prayer. Desire is an inward longing for something of which we are not possessed, of which we stand in need -- something which God has promised, and which may be secured by an earnest supplication of His throne of grace.

Spiritual desire, carried to a higher degree, is the evidence of the new birth. It is born in the renewed soul:

> *"As newborn babes, desire the sincere*
> *milk of the word, that ye may grow*
> *thereby."*

The absence of this holy desire in the heart is presumptive proof, either of a decline in spiritual ecstasy, or, that the new birth has never taken place.

> *"Blessed are they which do hunger and*
> *thirst after righteousness: for they shall*
> *be filled."*

These heaven-given appetites are the proof of a renewed heart, the evidence of a stirring spiritual life. Physical appetites are the attributes of a living body, not of a corpse, and spiritual desires belong to a soul made alive to God. And as the renewed soul hungers and thirsts after righteousness, these holy inward desires break out into earnest, supplicating prayer.

In prayer, we are shut up to the Name, merit and intercessory virtue of Jesus Christ, our great High Priest. Probing down, below the accompanying conditions and forces in prayer, we come to its vital basis, which is seated in the human heart. It is not simply our need; it is the heart's yearning for what we need, and for which we feel impelled to pray. Desire is the will in action; a strong, conscious longing, excited in the inner nature, for some great good. Desire exalts the object of its longing, and fixes the mind on it. It has choice, and fixedness, and flame in it, and prayer, based thereon, is explicit and specific. It knows its need, feels and sees the thing that will meet it, and hastens to acquire it.

Holy desire is much helped by devout contemplation. Meditation on our spiritual need, and on God's readiness and ability to correct it, aids desire to grow. Serious thought engaged in before praying, increases desire, makes it more insistent, and tends to save us from the menace of private prayer -- wandering thought. We fail much more in desire, than in its outward expression. We retain the form, while the inner life fades and almost dies.

One might well ask, whether the feebleness of our desires for God, the Holy Spirit, and for all the fulness of Christ, is not the cause of our so little praying, and of our languishing in the exercise of prayer? Do we really feel these inward pantings of desire after heavenly treasures? Do the inbred groanings of desire stir our souls to mighty wrestlings? Alas for us! The fire burns altogether too low. The flaming heat of soul has been tempered down to a tepid lukewarmness. This, it should be remembered, was the central cause of the sad and desperate condition of the Laodicean Christians, of whom the awful condemnation is written that they were "rich, and increased in goods and *had need of nothing,*" and knew not that they "were wretched, and miserable, and poor, and blind."

Again: we might well inquire -- have we that desire which presses us to close communion with God, which is filled with unutterable burnings, and holds us there through the agony of an intense and soul-stirred supplication? Our hearts need much to be worked over, not only to get the evil out of them, but to get the good into them. And the foundation and inspiration to the incoming good, is strong, propelling desire. This holy and fervid flame in the soul awakens the interest of heaven, attracts the attention of God, and places at the disposal of those who exercise it, the exhaustless riches of Divine grace.

The dampening of the flame of holy desire, is destructive of the vital and aggressive forces in church life. God requires to be represented by a fiery Church, or He is not in any proper sense, represented at all. God, Himself, is all on fire, and His Church, if it is to be like Him, must also be at white heat. The great and eternal interests of heaven-born, God-given religion are the only things about which His Church can afford to be on fire. Yet holy zeal need not to be fussy in order to be consuming. Our Lord was the incarnate antithesis of nervous excitability, the absolute opposite of intolerant or clamorous declamation, yet the zeal of God's house consumed Him; and the world is still feeling the glow of His fierce, consuming flame and responding to it, with an ever-increasing readiness and an ever-enlarging response.

A lack of ardour in prayer, is the sure sign of a lack of depth and of intensity of desire; and the absence of intense desire is a sure sign of God's absence from the heart! To abate fervour is to retire from God. He can, and does, tolerate many things in the way of infirmity and error in His children. He can, and will pardon sin when the penitent prays, but two things are intolerable to Him -- insincerity and lukewarmness. Lack of heart and lack of heat are two things He loathes, and to the Laodiceans He said, in terms of unmistakable severity and condemnation:

> *"I would thou wert cold or hot. So then*
> *because thou art lukewarm, and neither*
> *cold nor hot, I will spue thee out of My*
> *mouth."*

This was God's expressed judgment on the lack of fire in one of the Seven Churches, and it is His indictment against individual Christians for the fatal want of sacred zeal. In prayer, fire is the motive power. Religious principles which do not emerge in flame, have neither force nor effect. Flame is the wing on which faith ascends; fervency is the soul of prayer. It was the "fervent, effectual prayer" which availed much. Love is kindled in a flame, and ardency is its life. Flame is the air which true Christian experience breathes. It feeds on fire; it can withstand anything, rather than a feeble flame; and it dies, chilled and starved to its vitals, when the surrounding atmosphere is frigid or lukewarm.

True prayer, *must* be aflame. Christian life and character need to be all on fire. Lack of spiritual heat creates more infidelity than lack of faith. Not to be consumingly interested about the things of heaven, is not to be interested in them at all. The fiery souls are those who conquer in the day of battle, from whom the kingdom of heaven suffereth violence, and who take it by force. The citadel of God is taken only by those, who storm it in dreadful earnestness, who besiege it, with fiery, unabated zeal.

Nothing short of being red hot for God, can keep the glow of heaven in our hearts, these chilly days. The early Methodists had no heating apparatus in their churches. They declared that the flame in the pew and the fire in the pulpit must suffice to keep them warm. And we, of this hour, have need to have the live coal from God's altar and the consuming flame from heaven glowing in our hearts. This flame is not mental vehemence nor fleshy energy. It is Divine fire in the soul, intense, dross-consuming -- the very essence of the Spirit of God.

No erudition, no purity of diction, no width of mental outlook, no flowers of eloquence, no grace of person, can atone for lack of fire. Prayer ascends by fire. Flame gives prayer access as well as wings, acceptance as well as energy. There is no incense without fire; no prayer without flame.

Ardent desire is the basis of unceasing prayer. It is not a shallow, fickle inclination, but a strong yearning, an unquenchable ardour, which impregnates, glows, burns and fixes the heart. It is the flame of a present and active principle mounting up to God. It is ardour propelled by desire, that burns its way to the Throne of mercy, and gains its plea. It is the pertinacity of desire that gives triumph to the conflict, in a great struggle of prayer. It is the burden of a weighty desire that sobers, makes restless, and reduces to quietness the soul just emerged from its mighty wrestlings. It is the embracing character of desire which arms prayer with a thousand pleas, and robes it with an invincible courage and an all-conquering power.

The Syrophenician woman is an object lesson of desire, settled to its consistency, but invulnerable in its intensity and pertinacious boldness. The importunate widow represents desire gaining its end, through obstacles insuperable to feebler impulses.

Prayer is not the rehearsal of a mere performance; nor is it an indefinite, widespread clamour. Desire, while it kindles the soul, holds it to the object sought. Prayer is an indispensable phase of spiritual habit, but it ceases to be prayer when carried on by habit alone. It is depth and intensity of spiritual desire which give intensity and depth to prayer. The soul cannot be listless when some great desire fires and inflames it. The urgency of our desire holds us to the thing desired with a tenacity which refuses to be lessened or loosened; it stays and pleads and persists, and refuses to let go until the blessing has been vouchsafed.

> *"Lord, I cannot let Thee go, Till a blessing Thou bestow; Do not turn away Thy face; Mine's an urgent, pressing case."*

The secret of faint heartedness, lack of importunity, want of courage and strength in prayer, lies in the weakness of spiritual desire, while the non-observance of prayer is the fearful token of that desire having ceased to live. That soul has turned from God whose desire after Him no longer presses it to the inner chamber. There can be no successful praying without consuming desire. Of course there can be much *seeming* to pray, without desire of any kind.

Many things may be catalogued and much ground covered. But does desire compile the catalogue? Does desire map out the region to be covered? On the answer, hangs the issue of whether our petitioning be prating or prayer. Desire is intense, but narrow; it cannot spread itself over a wide area. It wants a few things, and wants them badly, so badly, that nothing but God's willingness to answer, can bring it easement or content.

Desire single-shots at its objective. There may be many things desired, but they are specifically and individually felt and expressed. David did not yearn for everything; nor did he allow his desires to spread out everywhere and hit nothing. Here is the way his desires ran and found expression:

> *"One thing have I desired of the Lord,*
> *that will I seek after; that I may dwell in*
> *the house of the Lord all the days of my*
> *life, to behold the beauty of the Lord, and*
> *to enquire in His temple."*

It is this singleness of desire, this definiteness of yearning, which counts in praying, and which drives prayer directly to core and centre of supply.

In the Beatitudes Jesus voiced the words which directly bear upon the innate desires of a renewed soul, and the promise that they will be granted: "Blessed are they that do hunger and thirst after righteousness, for they shall be filled."

This, then, is the basis of prayer which compels an answer -- that strong inward desire has entered into the spiritual appetite, and clamours to be satisfied. Alas for us! It is altogether too true and frequent, that our prayers operate in the arid region of a mere wish, or in the leafless area of a memorized prayer. Sometimes, indeed, our prayers are merely stereotyped expressions of set phrases, and conventional proportions, the freshness and life of which have departed long years ago.

Without desire, there is no burden of soul, no sense of need, no ardency, no vision, no strength, no glow of faith. There is no mighty pressure, no holding on to God, with a deathless, despairing grasp -- "I will not let Thee go, except Thou bless me." There is no utter self-abandonment, as there was with Moses, when, lost in the throes of a desperate, pertinacious, and all-consuming plea he cried: "Yet now, if Thou wilt forgive their sin; if not, blot me, I pray Thee, out of Thy book." Or, as there was with John Knox when he pleaded: "Give me Scotland, or I die!"

God draws mightily near to the praying soul. To see God, to know God, and to live for God -- these form the objective of all true praying. Thus praying is, after all, inspired to seek after God. Prayer-desire is inflamed to see God, to have clearer, fuller, sweeter and richer revelation of God. So to those who thus pray, the Bible becomes a *new* Bible, and Christ a new Saviour, by the light and revelation of the inner chamber.

We iterate and reiterate that burning desire -- enlarged and ever enlarging -- for the best, and most powerful gifts and graces of the Spirit of God, is the legitimate heritage of true and effectual praying. Self and service cannot be divorced -- cannot, possibly, be separated. More than that: desire must be made intensely personal, must be centered on God with an insatiable hungering and thirsting after Him and His righteousness. "My soul thirsteth for God, the living God." The indispensable requisite for all true praying is a deeply seated desire which seeks after God Himself, and remains unappeased, until the choicest gifts in heaven's bestowal, have been richly and abundantly vouchsafed.

V

PRAYER AND FERVENCY

"St. Teresa rose off her deathbed to finish her work. She inspected, with all her quickness of eye and love of order the whole of the house in which she had been carried to die. She saw everything put into its proper place, and every one answering to their proper order, after which she attended the divine offices of the day. She then went back to her bed, summoned her daughters around her . . . and, with the most penitential of David's penitential prayers upon her tongue, Teresa of Jesus went forth to meet her Bridegroom."

ALEXANDER WHYTE

PRAYER, without fervour, stakes nothing on the issue, because it has nothing to stake. It comes with empty hands. Hands, too, which are listless, as well as empty, which have never learned the lesson of clinging to the Cross.

Fervourless prayer has no heart in it; it is an empty thing, an unfit vessel. Heart, soul, and life, must find place in all real praying. Heaven must be made to feel the force of this crying unto God.

Paul was a notable example of the man who possessed a fervent spirit of prayer. His petitioning was all-consuming, centered immovably upon the object of his desire, and the God who was able to meet it.

Prayers must be red hot. It is the fervent prayer that is effectual and that availeth. Coldness of spirit hinders praying; prayer cannot live in a wintry atmosphere. Chilly surroundings freeze out petitioning; and dry up the springs of supplication. It takes fire to make prayers go. Warmth of soul creates an atmosphere favourable to prayer, because it is favourable to fervency. By flame, prayer ascends to heaven. Yet fire is not fuss, nor heat, noise. Heat is intensity -- something that glows and burns. Heaven is a mighty poor market for ice.

God wants warm-hearted servants. The Holy Spirit comes *as a fire*, to dwell in us; we are to be baptized, with the Holy Ghost and with fire. Fervency is warmth of soul. A phlegmatic temperament is abhorrent to vital experience. If our religion does not set us on fire, it is because we have frozen hearts. God dwells in a flame; the Holy Ghost descends in fire. To be absorbed in God's will, to be so greatly in earnest about doing it that our whole being takes fire, is the qualifying condition of the man who would engage in effectual prayer.

Our Lord warns us against feeble praying. "Men ought always to pray," He declares, "and not to faint." That means, that we are to possess sufficient fervency to carry us through the severe and long periods of pleading prayer. Fire makes one alert and vigilant, and brings him off, more than conqueror. The atmosphere about us is too heavily charged with resisting forces for limp or languid prayers to make headway. It takes heat, and fervency and meteoric fire, to push through, to the upper heavens, where God dwells with His saints, in light.

Many of the great Bible characters were notable examples of fervency of spirit when seeking God. The Psalmist declares with great earnestness:

> *"My soul breaketh for the longing that*
> *it hath unto Thy judgments at all*
> *times."*

What strong desires of heart are here! What earnest soul longings for the Word of the living God!

An even greater fervency is expressed by him in another place:

> *"As the hart panteth after the water*
> *brooks, so panteth my soul after Thee, O*
> *God. My soul thirsteth for God, for the*
> *living God: when shall I come and*
> *appear before God?"*

That is the word of a man who lived in a state of grace, which had been deeply and supernaturally wrought in his soul.

Fervency before God counts in the hour of prayer, and finds a speedy and rich reward at His hands. The Psalmist gives us this statement of what God had done for the king, as his heart turned toward his Lord:

> *"Thou hast given him his heart's desire,*
> *and hast not withholden the request of*
> *his lips."*

At another time, he thus expresses himself directly to God in preferring his request:

> *"Lord, all my desire is before Thee; and*
> *my groaning is not hid from Thee."*

What a cheering thought! Our inward groanings, our secret desires, our heart-longings, are not hidden from the eyes of Him with whom we have to deal in prayer.

The incentive to fervency of spirit before God, is precisely the same as it is for continued and earnest prayer. While fervency is not prayer, yet it derives from an earnest soul, and is precious in the sight of God. Fervency in prayer is the precursor of what God will do by way of answer. God stands pledged to give us the desire of our hearts in proportion to the fervency of spirit we exhibit, when seeking His face in prayer.

Fervency has its seat in the heart, not in the brain, nor in the intellectual faculties of the mind. Fervency therefore, is not an expression of the intellect. Fervency of spirit is something far transcending poetical fancy or sentimental imagery. It is something else besides mere preference, the contrasting of like with dislike. Fervency is the throb and gesture of the emotional nature.

It is not in our power, perhaps, to create fervency of spirit at will, but we can pray God to implant it. It is ours, then, to nourish and cherish it, to guard it against extinction, to prevent its abatement or decline. The process of personal salvation is not only to pray, to express our desires to God, but to acquire a fervent spirit and seek, by all proper means, to cultivate it. It is never out of place to pray God to beget within us, and to keep alive the spirit of fervent prayer.

Fervency has to do with God, just as prayer has to do with Him. Desire has always an objective. If we desire at all, we desire *something*. The degree of fervency with which we fashion our spiritual desires, will always serve to determine the earnestness of our praying. In this relation, Adoniram Judson says:

> *"A travailing spirit, the throes of a great burdened desire, belongs to prayer. A fervency strong enough to drive away sleep, which devotes and inflames the spirit, and which retires all earthly ties, all this belongs to wrestling, prevailing prayer. The Spirit, the power, the air, and food of prayer is in such a spirit."*

Prayer must be clothed with fervency, strength and power. It is the force which, centered on God, determines the outlay of Himself for earthly good. Men who are fervent in spirit are bent on attaining to righteousness, truth, grace, and all other sublime and powerful graces which adorn the character of the authentic, unquestioned child of God.

God once declared, by the mouth of a brave prophet, to a king who, at one time, had been true to God, but, by the incoming of success and material prosperity, had lost his faith, the following message:

> *"The eyes of the Lord run to and fro throughout the whole earth, to shew Himself strong in the behalf of them whose heart is perfect toward Him. Herein hast thou done foolishly; therefore, from henceforth thou shalt have wars."*

God had heard Asa's prayer in early life, but disaster came and trouble was sent, because he had given up the life of prayer and simple faith.

In Romans 15:30, we have the word, "strive," occurring, in the request which Paul made for prayerful cooperation.

In Colossians 4:12, we have the same word, but translated differently: "Epaphras always labouring fervently for you in prayer." Paul charged the Romans to "strive together with him in prayer," that is, to help him in his struggle of prayer. The word means to enter into a contest, to fight against adversaries. It means, moreover, to engage with fervent zeal to endeavour to obtain.

These recorded instances of the exercise and reward of faith, give us easily to see that, in almost every instance, faith was blended with trust until it is not too much to say that the former was swallowed up in the latter. It is hard to properly distinguish the specific activities of these two qualities, faith and trust. But there is a point, beyond all peradventure, at which faith is relieved of its burden, so to speak; where trust comes along and says: "You have done your part, the rest is mine!"

In the incident of the barren fig tree, our Lord transfers the marvellous power of faith to His disciples. To their exclamation, "How soon is the fig tree withered alway!" He said:

"If ye have faith, and doubt not, ye shall not only do this which is done to the fig tree, but also if ye shall say unto this mountain, Be thou removed, and be thou cast into the sea; it shall be done. And all things, whatsoever ye shall ask in prayer, believing, ye shall receive."

When a Christian believer attains to faith of such magnificent proportions as these, he steps into the realm of implicit trust. He stands without a tremor on the apex of his spiritual outreaching. He has attained faith's veritable top stone which is unswerving, unalterable, unalienable trust in the power of the living God.

VI

PRAYER AND IMPORTUNITY

"How glibly we talk of praying without ceasing! Yet we are quite apt to quit, if our prayer remained unanswered but one week or month! We assume that by a stroke of His arm or an action of His will, God will give us what we ask. It never seems to dawn on us, that He is the Master of nature, as of grace, and that, sometimes He chooses one way, and sometimes another in which to do His work. It takes years, sometimes, to answer a prayer and when it is answered, and we look backward we can see that it did. But God knows all the time, and it is His will that we pray, and pray, and still pray, and so come to know, indeed and of a truth, what it is to pray without ceasing."

ANON

OUR Lord Jesus declared that "men ought always to pray and not to faint," and the parable in which His words occur, was taught with the intention of saving men from faint-heartedness and weakness in prayer. Our Lord was seeking to teach that laxity must be guarded against, and persistence fostered and encouraged. There can be no two opinions regarding the importance of the exercise of this indispensable quality in our praying.

Importunate prayer is a mighty movement of the soul toward God. It is a stirring of the deepest forces of the soul, toward the throne of heavenly grace. It is the ability to hold on, press on, and wait. Restless desire, restful patience, and strength of grasp are all embraced in it. It is not an incident, or a performance, but a passion of soul. It is not a want, half-needed, but a sheer necessity.

The wrestling quality in importunate prayers does not spring from physical vehemence or fleshly energy. It is not an impulse of energy, not a mere earnestness of soul; it is an inwrought force, a faculty implanted and aroused by the Holy Spirit. Virtually, it is the intercession of the Spirit of God, in us; it is, moreover, "the effectual, fervent prayer, which availeth much." The Divine Spirit informing every element within us, with the energy of His own striving, is the essence of the importunity which urges our praying at the mercy-seat, to continue until the fire falls and the blessing descends. This wrestling in prayer may not be boisterous nor vehement, but quiet, tenacious and urgent. Silent, it may be, when there are no visible outlets for its mighty forces.

Nothing distinguishes the children of God so clearly and strongly as prayer. It is the one infallible mark and test of being a Christian. Christian people are prayerful, the worldly-minded, prayerless. Christians call on God; worldlings ignore God, and call not on His Name. But even the Christian had need to cultivate continual prayer. Prayer must be habitual, but much more than a habit. It is duty, yet one which rises far above, and goes beyond the ordinary implications of the term. It is the expression of a relation to God, a yearning for Divine communion. It is the outward and upward flow of the inward life toward its original fountain. It is an assertion of the soul's paternity, a claiming of the sonship, which links man to the Eternal.

Prayer has everything to do with moulding the soul into the image of God, and has everything to do with enhancing and enlarging the measure of Divine grace. It has everything to do with bringing the soul into complete communion with God. It has everything to do with enriching, broadening and maturing the soul's experience of God. That man cannot possibly be called a Christian, who does not pray. By no possible pretext can he claim any right to the term, nor its implied significance. If he do not pray, he is a sinner, pure and simple, for prayer is the only way in which the soul of man can enter into fellowship and communion with the Source of all Christlike spirit and energy. Hence, if he pray not, he is not of the household of faith.

In this study however, we turn our thought to one phase of prayer -- that of importunity; the pressing of our desires upon God with urgency and perseverance; the praying with that tenacity and tension which neither relaxes nor ceases until its plea is heard, and its cause is won.

He who has clear views of God, and Scriptural conceptions of the Divine character; who appreciates his privilege of approach unto God; who understands his inward need of all that God has for him -- that man will be solicitous, outspoken and importunate. In Holy Writ, the duty of prayer, itself, is advocated in terms which are only barely stronger than those in which the necessity for its importunity is set forth. The praying which influences God is declared to be that of the fervent, effectual outpouring of a righteous man. That is to say, it is prayer on fire, having no feeble, flickering flame, no momentary flash, but shining with a vigorous and steady glow.

The repeated intercessions of Abraham for the salvation of Sodom and Gomorrah present an early example of the necessity for, and benefit deriving from importunate praying. Jacob, wrestling all night with the angel, gives significant emphasis to the power of a dogged perseverance in praying, and shows how, in things spiritual, importunity succeeds, just as effectively as it does in matters relating to time and sense.

As we have noted, elsewhere, Moses prayed forty days and forty nights, seeking to stay the wrath of God against Israel, and his example and success are a stimulus to present-day faith in its darkest hour. Elijah repeated and urged his prayer seven times ere the raincloud appeared above the horizon, heralding the success of his prayer and the victory of his faith. On one occasion Daniel though faint and weak, pressed his case three weeks, ere the answer and the blessing came.

Many nights during His earthly life did the blessed Saviour spend in prayer. In Gethsemane He presented the same petition, three times, with unabated, urgent, yet submissive importunity, which involved every element of His soul, and issued in tears and bloody sweat. His life crises were distinctly marked, his life victories all won, in hours of importunate prayer. And the servant is not greater than his Lord.

The Parable of the Importunate Widow is a classic of insistent prayer. We shall do well to refresh our remembrance of it, at this point in our study:

> *"And He spake a parable unto them to this end, that men ought always to pray, and not to faint; saying, There was in a city a judge, which feared not God, neither regarded man; and there was a widow in that city; and she came unto him, saying, Avenge me of my adversary. And he would not for a while; but afterward he said within himself, Though I fear not God nor regard man; yet because this widow troubleth me, I will avenge her, lest by her continual coming she weary me. And the Lord said, Hear what the unjust judge saith. And shall not God avenge His own elect, which cry day and night unto Him, though He bear long with them? I tell you He will avenge them speedily."*

This parable stresses the central truth of importunate prayer. The widow presses her case till the unjust judge yields. If this parable does not teach the necessity for importunity, it has neither point nor instruction in it. Take this one thought away, and you have nothing left worth recording. Beyond all cavil, Christ intended it to stand as an evidence of the need that exists, for insistent prayer.

We have the same teaching emphasized in the incident of the Syrophenician woman, who came to Jesus on behalf of her daughter. Here, importunity is demonstrated, not as a stark impertinence, but as with the persuasive habiliments of humility, sincerity, and fervency. We are given a glimpse of a woman's clinging faith, a woman's bitter grief, and a woman's spiritual insight. The Master went over into that Sidonian country in order that this truth might be mirrored for all time -- there is no plea so efficacious as importunate prayer, and none to which God surrenders Himself so fully and so freely.

The importunity of this distressed mother, won her the victory, and materialized her request. Yet instead of being an offence to the Saviour, it drew from Him a word of wonder, and glad surprise. "O woman, great is thy faith! Be it unto thee, even as thou wilt."

He prays not at all, who does not press his plea. Cold prayers have no claim on heaven, and no hearing in the courts above. Fire is the life of prayer, and heaven is reached by flaming importunity rising in an ascending scale.

Reverting to the case of the importunate widow, we see that her widowhood, her friendlessness, and her weakness counted for nothing with the unjust judge. Importunity was everything. "Because this widow *troubleth* me," he said, "I will avenge her speedily, lest she weary me." Solely because the widow imposed upon the time and attention of the unjust judge, her case was won.

God waits patiently as, day and night, His elect cry unto Him. He is moved by their requests a thousand times more than was this unjust judge. A limit is set to His tarrying, by the importunate praying of His people, and the answer richly given. God finds faith in His praying child -- the faith which stays and cries -- and He honours it by permitting its further exercise, to the end that it is strengthened and enriched. Then He rewards it by granting the burden of its plea, in plenitude and finality.

The case of the Syrophenician woman previously referred to is a notable instance of successful importunity, one which is eminently encouraging to all who would pray successfully. It was a remarkable instance of insistence and perseverance to ultimate victory, in the face of almost insuperable obstacles and hindrances. But the woman surmounted them all by heroic faith and persistent spirit that were as remarkable as they were successful. Jesus had gone over into her country, "and would have no man know it." But she breaks through His purpose, violates His privacy, attracts His attention, and pours out to Him a poignant appeal of need and faith. Her heart was in her prayer.

At first, Jesus appears to pay no attention to her agony, and ignores her cry for relief. He gives her neither eye, nor ear, nor word. Silence, deep and chilling, greets her impassioned cry. But she is not turned aside, nor disheartened. She holds on. The disciples, offended at her unseemly clamour, intercede for her, but are silenced by the Lord's declaring that the woman is entirely outside the scope of His mission and His ministry.

But neither the failure of the disciples to gain her a hearing nor the knowledge -- despairing in its very nature -- that she is barred from the benefits of His mission, daunt her, and serve only to lend intensity and increased boldness to her approach to Christ. She came closer, cutting her prayer in twain, and falling at His feet, worshipping Him, and making her daughter's case her own cries, with pointed brevity -- "Lord, help me!" This last cry won her case; her daughter was healed in the self-same hour. Hopeful, urgent, and unwearied, she stays near the Master, insisting and praying until the answer is given. What a study in importunity, in earnestness, in persistence, promoted and propelled under conditions which would have disheartened any but an heroic, a constant soul.

In these parables of importunate praying, our Lord sets forth, for our information and encouragement, the serious difficulties which stand in the way of prayer. At the same time He teaches that importunity conquers all untoward circumstances and gets to itself a victory over a whole host of hindrances. He teaches, moreover, that an answer to prayer is conditional upon the amount of faith that goes to the petition. To test this, He delays the answer. The superficial pray-er subsides into silence, when the answer is delayed. But the man of prayer hangs on, and on. The Lord recognizes and honours his faith, and gives him a rich and abundant answer to his faith-evidencing, importunate prayer.

VII

PRAYER AND IMPORTUNITY (Continued)

"Two-thirds of the praying we do, is for that which would give us the greatest possible pleasure to receive. It is a sort of spiritual self-indulgence in which we engage, and as a consequence is the exact opposite of self-discipline. God knows all this, and keeps His children asking. In process of time -- His time -- our petitions take on another aspect, and we, another spiritual approach. God keeps us praying until, in His wisdom, He deigns to answer. And no matter how long it may be before He speaks, it is, even then, far earlier than we have a right to expect or hope to deserve."

ANON

THE tenor of Christ's teachings, is to declare that men are to pray earnestly -- to pray with an earnestness that cannot be denied. Heaven has harkening ears only for the whole-hearted, and the deeply-earnest. Energy, courage, and persistent perseverance must back the prayers which heaven respects, and God hears. All these qualities of soul, so essential to effectual praying, are brought out in the parable of the man who went to his friend for bread, at midnight. This man entered on his errand with confidence. Friendship promised him success. His plea was pressing: of a truth, he could not go back empty-handed. The flat refusal chagrined and surprised him. Here even friendship failed! But there was something to be tried yet -- stern resolution, set, fixed determination. He would stay and press his demand until the door was opened, and the request granted. This he proceeded to do, and by dint of importunity secured what ordinary solicitation had failed to obtain.

The success of this man, achieved in the face of a flat denial, was used by the Saviour to illustrate the necessity for insistence in supplicating the throne of heavenly grace. When the answer is not immediately given, the praying Christian must gather courage at each delay, and advance in urgency till the answer comes which is assured, if he have but the faith to press his petition with vigorous faith.

Laxity, faint-heartedness, impatience, timidity will be fatal to our prayers. Awaiting the onset of our importunity and insistence, is the Father's heart, the Father's hand, the Father's infinite power, the Father's infinite willingness to hear and give to His children.

Importunate praying is the earnest, inward movement of the heart toward God. It is the throwing of the entire force of the spiritual man into the exercise of prayer. Isaiah lamented that no one stirred himself, to take hold of God. Much praying was done in Isaiah's time, but it was too easy, indifferent and complacent. There were no mighty movements of souls toward God. There was no array of sanctified energies bent on reaching and grappling with God, to draw from Him the treasures of His grace. Forceless prayers have no power to overcome difficulties, no power to win marked results, or to gain complete victories. We must win God, ere we can win our plea.

Isaiah looked forward with hopeful eyes to the day when religion would flourish, when there would be times of real praying. When those times came, the watchmen would not abate their vigilance, but cry day and night, and those, who were the Lord's remembrancers, would give Him no rest. Their urgent, persistent efforts would keep all spiritual interests engaged, and make increasing drafts on God's exhaustless treasures.

Importunate praying never faints nor grows weary; it is never discouraged; it never yields to cowardice, but is buoyed up and sustained by a hope that knows no despair, and a faith which will not let go. Importunate praying has patience to wait and strength to continue. It never prepares itself to quit praying, and declines to rise from its knees until an answer is received.

The familiar, yet heartening words of that great missionary, Adoniram Judson, is the testimony of a man who was importunate at prayer. He says:

> *"I was never deeply interested in any object, never prayed sincerely and earnestly for it, but that it came at some time, no matter how distant the day. Somehow, in some shape, probably the last I would have devised, it came."*

"Ask, and ye shall receive. Seek, and ye shall find. Knock, and it shall be opened unto you." These are the ringing challenges of our Lord in regard to prayer, and His intimation that true praying must stay, and advance in effort and urgency, till the prayer is answered, and the blessing sought, received.

In the three words ask, seek, knock, in the order in which He places them, Jesus urges the necessity of importunity in prayer. Asking, seeking, knocking, are ascending rounds in the ladder of successful prayer. No principle is more definitely enforced by Christ than that prevailing prayer must have in it the quality which waits and perseveres, the courage that never surrenders, the patience which never grows tired, the resolution that never wavers.

In the parable preceding that of the Friend at Midnight, a most significant and instructive lesson in this respect is outlined. Indomitable courage, ceaseless pertinacity, fixity of purpose, chief among the qualities included in Christ's estimate of the highest and most successful form of praying.

Importunity is made up of intensity, perseverance, patience and persistence. The seeming delay in answering prayer is the ground and the demand of importunity. In the first recorded instance of a miracle being wrought upon one who was blind, as given by Matthew, we have an illustration of the way in which our Lord appeared not to hearken at once to those who sought Him. But the two blind men continue their crying, and follow Him with their continual petition, saying, "Thou Son of David, have mercy on us." But He answered them not, and passed into the house. Yet the needy ones followed Him, and, finally, gained their eyesight and their plea.

The case of blind Bartimaeus is a notable one in many ways. Especially is it remarkable for the show of persistence which this blind man exhibited in appealing to our Lord. If it be -- as it seems -- that his first crying was done as Jesus entered into Jericho, and that he continued it until Jesus came out of the place, it is all the stronger an illustration of the necessity of importunate prayer and the success which comes to those who stake their all on Christ, and give Him no peace until He grants them their hearts' desire.

Mark puts the whole incident graphically before us. At first, Jesus seems not to hear. The crowd rebukes the noisy clamour of Bartimaeus. Despite the seeming unconcern of our Lord, however, and despite the rebuke of an impatient and quick-tempered crowd, the blind beggar still cries, and increases the loudness of his cry, until Jesus is impressed and moved. Finally, the crowd, as well as Jesus, hearken to the beggar's plea and declare in favour of his cause. He gains his case. His importunity avails even in the face of apparent neglect on the part of Jesus, and despite opposition and rebuke from the surrounding populace. His persistence won where half-hearted indifference would surely have failed.

Faith has its province, in connection with prayer, and, of course, has its inseparable association with importunity. But the latter quality *drives* the prayer to the believing point. A persistent spirit brings a man to the place where faith takes hold, claims and appropriates the blessing.

The imperative necessity of importunate prayer is plainly set forth in the Word of God, and needs to be stated and re-stated today. We are apt to overlook this vital truth. Love of ease, spiritual indolence, religious slothfulness, all operate against this type of petitioning. Our praying, however, needs to be pressed and pursued with an energy that never tires, a persistency which will not be denied, and a courage which never fails.

We have need, too, to give thought to that mysterious fact of prayer -- the certainty that there will be delays, denials, and seeming failures, in connection with its exercise. We are to prepare for these, to brook them, and cease not in our urgent praying. Like a brave soldier, who, as the conflict grows sterner, exhibits a superior courage than in the earlier stages of the battle; so does the praying Christian, when delay and denial face him, increase his earnest asking, and ceases not until prayer prevail. Moses furnishes an illustrious example of importunity in prayer. Instead of allowing his nearness to God and his intimacy with Him to dispense with the necessity for importunity, he regards them as the better fitting him for its exercise. When Israel set up the golden calf, the wrath of God waxed fierce against them, and Jehovah, bent on executing justice, said to Moses when divulging what He purposed doing, "Let Me alone!" But Moses would *not* let Him alone. He threw himself down before the Lord in an agony of intercession in behalf of the sinning Israelites, and for forty days and nights, fasted and prayed. What a season of importunate prayer was that!

Jehovah was wroth with Aaron, also, who had acted as leader in this idolatrous business of the golden calf. But Moses prayed for Aaron as well as for the Israelites; had he not, both Israel and Aaron had perished, under the consuming fire of God's wrath.

That long season of pleading before God, left its mighty impress on Moses. He had been in close relation with God aforetime, but never did his character attain the greatness that marked it in the days and years following this long season of importunate intercession.

There can be no question but that importunate prayer moves God, and heightens human character! If we were more with God in this great ordinance of intercession, more brightly would our face shine, more richly endowed would life and service be, with the qualities which earn the goodwill of humanity, and bring glory to the Name of God.

VIII

PRAYER AND CHARACTER AND CONDUCT

"General Charles James Gordon, the hero of Khartum, was a truly Christian soldier. Shut up in the Sudanese town he gallantly held out for one year, but, finally, was overcome and slain. On his memorial in Westminster Abbey are these words, 'He gave his money to the poor; his sympathy to the sorrowing; his life to his country and his soul to God.'"

HOMER W. HODGE

PRAYER governs conduct and conduct makes character. Conduct, is what we do; character, is what we are. Conduct is the outward life. Character is the life unseen, hidden within, yet evidenced by that which *is* seen. Conduct is external, seen from without; character is internal -- operating within. In the economy of grace conduct is the offspring of character. Character is the state of the heart, conduct its outward expression. Character is the root of the tree, conduct, the fruit it bears.

Prayer is related to all the gifts of grace. To character and conduct its relation is that of a helper. Prayer helps to establish character and fashion conduct, and both for their successful continuance depend on prayer. There may be a certain degree of moral character and conduct independent of prayer, but there cannot be anything like distinctive religious character and Christian conduct without it. Prayer helps, where all other aids fail. The more we pray, the better we are, the purer and better our lives.

The very end and purpose of the atoning work of Christ is to create religious character and to make Christian conduct.

"Who gave Himself for us, that He might redeem us from all iniquity, and

> *purify unto Himself a peculiar people,*
> *zealous of good works."*

In Christ's teaching, it is not simply works of charity and deeds of mercy upon which He insists, but inward spiritual character. This much is demanded, and nothing short of it, will suffice.

In the study of Paul's Epistles, there is one thing which stands out, clearly and unmistakably -- the insistence on holiness of heart, and righteousness of life. Paul does not seek, so much, to promote what is termed "personal work," nor is the leading theme of his letters deeds of charity. It is the condition of the human heart and the blamelessness of the personal life, which form the burden of the writings of St. Paul.

Elsewhere in the Scriptures, too, it is character and conduct which are made preeminent. The Christian religion deals with men who are devoid of spiritual character, and unholy in life, and aims so to change them, that they become holy in heart and righteous in life. It aims to change bad men into good men; it deals with inward badness, and works to change it into inward goodness. And it is just here where prayer enters and demonstrates its wonderful efficacy and fruit. Prayer drives toward this specific end. In fact, without prayer, no such supernatural change in moral character, can ever be effected. For the change from badness to goodness is not wrought "by works of righteousness which we have done," but according to God's mercy, which saves us "by the washing of regeneration." And this marvellous change is brought to pass through earnest, persistent, faithful prayer. Any alleged form of Christianity, which does not effect this change in the hearts of men, is a delusion and a snare.

The office of prayer is to change the character and conduct of men, and in countless instances, has been wrought by prayer. At this point, prayer, by its credentials, has proved its divinity. And just as it is the office of prayer to effect this, so it is the prime work of the Church to take hold of evil men and make them good. Its mission is to change human nature, to change character, influence behaviour, to revolutionize conduct. The Church is presumed to be righteous, and should be engaged in turning men to righteousness.

The Church is God's manufactory on earth, and its primary duty is to create and foster righteousness of character. This is its very first business. Primarily, its work is not to acquire members, nor amass numbers, nor aim at money-getting, nor engage in deeds of charity and works of mercy, but to produce righteousness of character, and purity of the outward life.

A product reflects and partakes of the character of the manufactory which makes it. A righteous Church with a righteous purpose makes righteous men. Prayer produces cleanliness of heart and purity of life. It can produce nothing else. Unrighteous conduct is born of prayerlessness; the two go hand-in-hand. Prayer and sinning cannot keep company with each other. One, or the other, must, of necessity, stop. Get men to pray, and they will quit sinning, because prayer creates a distaste for sinning, and so works upon the heart, that evil-doing becomes repugnant, and the entire nature lifted to a reverent contemplation of high and holy things.

Prayer is based on character. What we are with God gauges our influence with Him. It was the inner character, not the outward seeming, of such men as Abraham, Job, David, Moses and all others, who had such great influence with God in the days of old. And, today, it is not so much our words, as what we really are, which weighs with God. Conduct affects character, of course, and counts for much in our praying. At the same time, character affects conduct to a far greater extent, and has a superior influence over prayer. Our inner life not only gives colour to our praying, but body, as well. Bad living means bad praying and, in the end, no praying at all. We pray feebly because we live feebly. The stream of prayer cannot rise higher than the fountain of living. The force of the inner chamber is made up of the energy which flows from the confluent streams of living. And the weakness of living grows out of the shallowness and shoddiness of character.

Feebleness of living reflects its debility and langour in the praying hours. We simply cannot talk to God, strongly, intimately, and confidently unless we are living for Him, faithfully and truly. The prayer-closet cannot become sanctified unto God, when the life is alien to His precepts and purpose. We must learn this lesson well -- that righteous character and Christlike conduct give us a peculiar and preferential standing in prayer before God. His holy Word gives special emphasis to the part conduct has in imparting value to our praying when it declares:

> *"Then shalt thou call and the Lord shall*
> *answer; thou shalt cry, and He shall*
> *say, Here I am; if thou take away from*
> *the midst of thee the yoke, the putting*
> *forth the finger, and speaking vanity."*

The wickedness of Israel and their heinous practices were definitely cited by Isaiah, as the reason why God would turn His ears away from their prayers:

> *"And when ye spread forth your hands,*
> *I will hide mine eyes from you: yea,*
> *when ye make many prayers, I will not*
> *hear: your hands are full of blood."*

The same sad truth was declared by the Lord through the mouth of Jeremiah:

> *"Therefore, pray not thou for this*
> *people, neither lift up a cry or prayer for*
> *them; for I will not hear them in the*
> *time that they cry unto Me for their*
> *trouble."*

Here, it is plainly stated, that unholy conduct is a bar to successful praying, just as it is clearly intimated that, in order to have full access to God in prayer, there must be a total abandonment of conscious and premeditated sin.

We are enjoined to pray, "lifting up holy hands, without wrath and doubting," and must pass the time of our sojourning here, in a rigorous abstaining from evil if we are to retain our privilege of calling upon the Father. We cannot, by any process, divorce praying from conduct.

*"Whatsoever we ask, we receive of Him,
because we keep His commandments,
and do those things which are pleasing
in His sight."*

And James declares roundly that men ask and receive not, because they ask amiss, and seek only the gratification of selfish desires.

Our Lord's injunction, "Watch ye, and pray always," is to cover and guard all our conduct, so that we may come to our inner chamber with all its force secured by a vigilant guard kept over our lives.

*"And take heed to yourselves, lest at
any time your hearts be overcharged
with surfeiting, and drunkenness, and
cares of this life, and so that day come
upon you unawares."*

Quite often, Christian experience founders on the rock of conduct. Beautiful theories are marred by ugly lives. The most difficult thing about piety, as it is the most impressive, is to be able to live it. It is the life which counts, and our praying suffers, as do other phases of our religious experience, from bad living.

In primitive times preachers were charged to preach by their lives, or not to preach at all. So, today, Christians, everywhere, ought to be charged to pray by their lives, or not to pray at all. The most effective preaching, is not that which is heard from the pulpit, but that which is proclaimed quietly, humbly and consistently; which exhibits its excellencies in the home, and in the community. Example preaches a far more effective sermon than precept. The best preaching, even in the pulpit, is that which is fortified by godly living, in the preacher, himself. The most effective work done by the pew is preceded by, and accompanied with, holiness of life, separation from the world, severance from sin. Some of the strongest appeals are made with mute lips -- by godly fathers and saintly mothers who, around the fireside, feared God, loved His cause, and daily exhibited to their children and others about them, the beauties and excellencies of Christian life and conduct.

The best-prepared, most eloquent sermon can be marred and rendered ineffective, by questionable practices in the preacher. The most active church worker can have the labour of his hands vitiated by worldliness of spirit and inconsistency of life. Men preach by their lives, not by their words, and sermons are delivered, not so much in, and from a pulpit, as in tempers, actions, and the thousand and one incidents which crowd the pathway of daily life.

Of course, the prayer of repentance is acceptable to God. He delights in hearing the cries of penitent sinners. But repentance involves not only sorrow for sin, but the turning away from wrongdoing, and the learning to do well. A repentance which does not produce a change in character and conduct, is a mere sham, which should deceive nobody. Old things *must* pass away, all things *must* become new.

Praying, which does not result in right thinking and right living, is a farce. We have missed the whole office of prayer if it fail to purge character and rectify conduct. We have failed entirely to apprehend the virtue of prayer, if it bring not about the revolutionizing of the life. In the very nature of things, we must quit praying, or our bad conduct. Cold, formal praying may exist side by side, with bad conduct, but such praying, in the estimation of God, is no praying at all. Our praying advances in power, just in so far as it rectifies the life. Growing in purity and devotion to God will be a more prayerful life.

The character of the inner life is a condition of effectual praying. As is the life, so will the praying be. An inconsistent life obstructs praying and neutralizes what little praying we may do. Always, it is "the prayer of the righteous man which availeth much." Indeed, one may go further and assert, that it is only the prayer of the righteous which avails anything at all -- at any time. To have an eye to God's glory; to be possessed by an earnest desire to please Him in all our ways; to possess hands busy in His service; to have feet swift to run in the way of His commandments -- these give weight and influence and power to prayer, and secure an audience with God. The incubus of our lives often breaks the force of our praying, and, not unfrequently, are as doors of brass, in the face of prayer.

Praying must come out of a cleansed heart and be presented and urged with the "lifting up of holy hands." It must be fortified by a life aiming, unceasingly, to obey God, to attain conformity to the Divine law, and to come into submission to the Divine will.

Let it not be forgotten, that, while life is a condition of prayer, prayer is also the condition of righteous living. Prayer promotes righteous living, and is the one great aid to uprightness of heart and life. The fruit of real praying is right living. Praying sets him who prays to the great business of "working out his salvation with fear and trembling;" puts him to watching his temper, conversation and conduct; causes him to "walk circumspectly, redeeming the time;" enables him to "walk worthy of the vocation wherewith he is called, with all lowliness and meekness;" gives him a high incentive to pursue his pilgrimage consistently by "shunning every evil way, and walking in the good."

IX

PRAYER AND OBEDIENCE

"An obedience discovered itself in Fletcher of Madeley, which I wish I could describe or imitate. It produced in him a ready mind to embrace every cross with alacrity and pleasure. He had a singular love for the lambs of the flock, and applied himself with the greatest diligence to their instruction, for which he had a peculiar gift. . . . All his intercourse with me was so mingled with prayer and praise, that every employment, and every meal was, as it were, perfumed therewith."

JOHN WESLEY

UNDER the Mosaic law, obedience was looked upon as being "better than sacrifice, and to harken, than the fat of lambs." In Deuteronomy 5:29, Moses represents Almighty God declaring Himself as to this very quality in a manner which left no doubt as to the importance He laid upon its exercise. Referring to the waywardness of His people He cries:

> *"O that there were such a heart in them,*
> *that they would fear Me, and keep all*
> *My commandments always, that it*
> *might be well with them, and with their*
> *children after them."*

Unquestionably obedience is a high virtue, a soldier quality. To obey belongs, preeminently, to the soldier. It is his first and last lesson, and he must learn how to practice it all the time, without question, uncomplainingly. Obedience, moreover, is faith in action, and is the outflow as it is the very test of love. "He that hath My commandments and keepeth them, he it is that loveth Me."

Furthermore: obedience is the conserver and the life of love.

> *"If ye keep My commandments," says*
> *Jesus, "ye shall abide in My love, even*
> *as   I   have   kept   My   Father's*
> *commandments and abide in His love."*

What a marvellous statement of the relationship created and maintained by obedience! The Son of God is held in the bosom of the Father's love, by virtue of His obedience! And the factor which enables the Son of God to ever abide in His Father's love is revealed in His own statement, "For I do, always, those things that please Him."

The gift of the Holy Spirit in full measure and in richer experience, depends upon loving obedience:

> *"If   ye   love   Me,   keep   My*
> *commandments," is the Master's word.*
> *"And I will pray the Father, and He*
> *shall give you another Comforter, that*
> *He may abide with you for ever."*

Obedience to God is a condition of spiritual thrift, inward satisfaction, stability of heart. "If ye be willing and obedient, ye shall eat the fruit of the land." Obedience opens the gates of the Holy City, and gives access to the tree of life.

> *"Blessed   are   they   that   do   His*
> *commandments,   that   they   may   have*
> *right to the tree of life, and may enter in*
> *through the gates, into the city."*

What is obedience? It is doing God's will: it is keeping His commandments. How many of the commandments constitute obedience? To keep half of them, and to break the other half -- is that real obedience? To keep all the commandments but one -- is that obedience? On this point, James the Apostle is most explicit:

"Whosoever shall keep the whole law," he declares, "and yet offend in one point, he is guilty of all."

The spirit which prompts a man to break one commandment is the spirit which may move him to break them all. God's commandments are a unit, and to break one strikes at the principle which underlies and runs through the whole. He who hesitates not to break a single commandment, would -- it is more than probable -- under the same stress, and surrounded by the same circumstances, break them all.

Universal obedience of the race is demanded. Nothing short of implicit obedience will satisfy God, and the keeping of all His commandments is the demonstration of it that God requires. But can we keep all of God's commandments? Can a man receive moral ability such as enables him to obey every one of them? Certainly he can. By every token, man can, through prayer, obtain ability to do this very thing.

Does God give commandments which men cannot obey? Is He so arbitrary, so severe, so unloving, as to issue commandments which cannot be obeyed? The answer is that in all the annals of Holy Scripture, not a single instance is recorded of God having commanded any man to do a thing, which was beyond his power. Is God so unjust and so inconsiderate as to require of man that which he is unable to render? Surely not. To infer it, is to slander the character of God.

Let us ponder this thought, a moment: Do earthly parents require of their children duties which they cannot perform? Where is the father who would think, even, of being so unjust, and so tyrannical? Is God less kind and just than faulty, earthly parents? Are they better and more just than a perfect God? How utterly foolish and untenable a thought!

In principle, obedience to God is the same quality as obedience to earthly parents. It implies, in general effect, the giving up of one's own way, and following that of another; the surrendering of the will to the will of another; the submission of oneself to the authority and requirements of a parent. Commands, either from our heavenly Father or from our earthly father, are love-directing, and all such commands are in the best interests of those who are commanded.

God's commands are issued neither in severity nor tyranny. They are always issued in love and in our interests, and so it behooves us to heed and obey them. In other words, and appraised at its lowest value -- God having issued His commands to us, in order to promote our good, it pays, therefore, to be obedient. Obedience brings its own reward. God has ordained it so, and since He has, even human reason can realize that He would never demand that which is out of our power to render.

Obedience is love, fulfilling every command, love expressing itself. Obedience, therefore, is not a hard demand made upon us, any more than is the service a husband renders his wife, or a wife renders her husband. Love delights to obey, and please whom it loves. There are no hardships in love. There may be exactions, but no irk. There are no impossible tasks for love.

With what simplicity and in what a matter-of-fact way does the Apostle John say: "And whatsoever we ask, we receive of Him, because we keep His commandments, and do those things which are pleasing in His sight."

This is obedience, running ahead of all and every command. It is love, obeying by anticipation. They greatly err, and even sin, who declare that men are bound to commit iniquity, either because of environment, or heredity, or tendency. God's commands are not grievous. Their ways are ways of pleasantness, and their paths peace. The task which falls to obedience is not a hard one. "For My yoke is easy, and My burden is light."

Far be it from our heavenly Father, to demand impossibilities of His children. It is possible to please Him in all things, for He is not hard to please. He is neither a hard master, nor an austere lord, "taking up that which he lays not down, and reaping that which he did not sow." Thank God, it is possible for every child of God, to please his heavenly Father! It is really much easier to please Him than to please men. Moreover, we may *know* when we please Him. This is the witness of the Spirit -- the inward Divine assurance, given to all the children of God that they are doing their Father's will, and that their ways are well-pleasing in His sight.

God's commandments are righteous and founded in justice and wisdom. "Wherefore the law is holy, and the commandment holy and just and good." "Just and true are Thy ways, Thou King of saints." God's commandments, then, can be obeyed by all who seek supplies of grace which enable them to obey. These commandments *must* be obeyed. God's government is at stake. God's children are under obligation to obey Him; disobedience cannot be permitted. The spirit of rebellion is the very essence of sin. It is repudiation of God's authority, which God cannot tolerate. He never has done so, and a declaration of His attitude was part of the reason the Son of the Highest was made manifest among men:

> *"For what the law could not do, in that it was weak through the flesh, God sending His own Son in the likeness of sinful flesh, and for sin, condemned sin in the flesh: that the righteousness of the law might be fulfilled in us, who walk not after the flesh, but after the Spirit."*

If any should complain that humanity, under the fall, is too weak and helpless to obey these high commands of God, the reply is in order that, through the atonement of Christ, man is enabled to obey. The Atonement is God's Enabling Act. That which God works in us, in regeneration and through the agency of the Holy Spirit, bestows enabling grace sufficient for all that is required of us, under the Atonement. This grace is furnished without measure, in answer to prayer. So that, while God commands, He, at the same time, stands pledged to give us all necessary strength of will and grace of soul to meet His demands. This being true, man is without excuse for his disobedience and eminently censurable for refusing, or failing, to secure requisite grace, whereby he may serve the Lord with reverence, and with godly fear.

There is one important consideration those who declare it to be impossible to keep God's commandments strangely overlook, and that is the vital truth, which declares that through prayer and faith, man's nature is changed, and made partaker of the Divine nature; that there is taken out of him all reluctance to obey God, and that his natural inability to keep God's commandments, growing out of his fallen and helpless state, is gloriously removed. By this radical change which is wrought in his moral nature, a man receives power to obey God in every way, and to yield full and glad allegiance. Then he can say, "I delight to do Thy will, O my God." Not only is the rebellion incident to the natural man removed, but a heart which gladly obeys God's Word, blessedly received.

If it be claimed, that the unrenewed man, with all the disabilities of the Fall upon him, cannot obey God, there will be no denial. But to declare that, after one is renewed by the Holy Spirit, has received a new nature, and become a child of the King, he cannot obey God, is to assume a ridiculous attitude, and to display, moreover, a lamentable ignorance of the work and implications of the Atonement.

Implicit and perfect obedience is the state to which the man of prayer is called. "Lifting up holy hands, without wrath and doubting," is the condition of obedient praying. Here inward fidelity and love, together with outward cleanness are put down as concomitants of acceptable praying.

John gives the reason for answered prayer in the passage previously quoted: "And whatsoever we ask we receive of Him because we keep His commandments and do those things which are pleasing in His sight."

Seeing that the keeping of God's commandments is here set forth as the reason why He answers prayer, it is to be reasonably assumed that we *can* keep God's commandments, *can* do those things which are pleasing to Him. Would God make the keeping of His commandments a condition of effectual prayer, think you, if He knew we could not keep His statutes? Surely, surely not!

Obedience can ask with boldness at the Throne of grace, and those who exercise it are the only ones who *can* ask, after that fashion. The disobedient folk are timid in their approach and hesitant in their supplication. They are halted by reason of their wrong-doing. The requesting yet obedient child comes into the presence of his father with confidence and boldness. His very consciousness of obedience gives him courage and frees him from the dread born of disobedience.

To do God's will without demur, is the joy as it is the privilege of the successful praying-man. It is he who has clean hands and a pure heart, that can pray with confidence. In the Sermon on the Mount, Jesus said:

> *"Not every one that saith unto me,*
> *Lord, Lord, shall enter into the kingdom*
> *of heaven, but he that doeth the will of*
> *My Father which is in heaven."*

To this great deliverance may be added another:

> *"If ye keep My commandments ye shall*
> *abide in My love, even as I have kept my*
> *Father's commandments, and abide in*
> *His love."*

"The Christian's trade," says Luther, "is prayer." But the Christian has another trade to learn, before he proceeds to learn the secrets of the trade of prayer. He must learn well the trade of perfect obedience to the Father's will. Obedience follows love, and prayer follows obedience. The business of *real* observance of God's commandments inseparably accompanies the business of *real* praying.

One who has been disobedient may pray. He may pray for pardoning mercy and the peace of his soul. He may come to God's footstool with tears, with confession, with penitent heart, and God will hear him and answer his prayer. But this kind of praying does not belong to the child of God, but to the penitent sinner, who has no other way by which to approach God. It is the possession of the unjustified soul, not of him who has been saved and reconciled to God.

An obedient life helps prayer. It speeds prayer to the throne. God cannot help hearing the prayer of an obedient child. He always has heard His obedient children when they have prayed. Unquestioning obedience counts much in the sight of God, at the throne of heavenly grace. It acts like the confluent tides of many rivers, and gives volume and fulness of flow as well as power to the prayer chamber. An obedient life is not simply a reformed life. It is not the old life primed and painted anew nor a church-going life, nor a good veneering of activities. Neither is it an external conformation to the dictates of public morality. Far more than all this is combined in a truly obedient Christian, God-fearing life.

A life of full obedience; a life settled on the most intimate terms with God; where the will is in full conformity to God's will; where the outward life shows the fruit of righteousness -- such a life offers no bar to the inner chamber but rather, like Aaron and Hur, it lifts up and sustains the hands of prayer.

If you have an earnest desire to pray well, you must learn how to obey well. If you have a desire to learn to pray, then you must have an earnest desire to learn how to do God's will. If you desire to pray to God, you must first have a consuming desire to obey Him. If you would have free access to God in prayer, then every obstacle in the nature of sin or disobedience, must be removed. God delights in the prayers of obedient children. Requests coming from the lips of those who delight to do His will, reach His ears with great celerity, and incline Him to answer them with promptitude and abundance. In themselves, tears are not meritorious. Yet they have their uses in prayer. Tears should baptize our place of supplication. He who has never wept concerning his sins, has never really *prayed* over his sins. Tears, sometimes, is a penitent's only plea. But tears are for the past, for the sin and the wrongdoing. There is another step and stage, waiting to be taken. It is that of unquestioning obedience, and until it is taken, prayer for blessing and continued sustenance, will be of no avail.

Everywhere in Holy Scripture God is represented as disapproving of disobedience and condemning sin, and this is as true in the lives of His elect as it is in the lives of sinners. Nowhere does He countenance sin, or excuse disobedience. Always, God puts the emphasis upon obedience to His commands. Obedience to them brings blessing, disobedience meets with disaster. This is true, in the Word of God, from its beginning to its close. It is because of this, that the men of prayer, in Holy Writ, had such influence with God.

Obedient men, always, have been the closest to God. These are they who have prayed well and have received great things from God, who have brought great things to pass.

Obedience to God counts tremendously in the realm of prayer. This fact cannot be emphasized too much or too often. To plead for a religious faith which tolerates sinning, is to cut the ground from under the feet of effectual praying. To excuse sinning by the plea that obedience to God is not possible to unregenerate men, is to discount the character of the new birth, and to place men where effective praying is not possible. At one time Jesus broke out with a very pertinent and personal question, striking right to the core of disobedience, when He said: "Why call ye Me, Lord, Lord, and do not the things I say?"

He who would pray, must obey. He who would get anything out of his prayers, must be in perfect harmony with God. Prayer puts into those who sincerely pray a spirit of obedience, for the spirit of disobedience is not of God and belongs not to God's praying hosts.

An obedient life is a great help to prayer. In fact, an obedient life is a necessity to prayer, to the sort which accomplishes things. The absence of an obedient life makes prayer an empty performance, a mere misnomer. A penitent sinner seeks pardon and salvation and has an answer to his prayers even with a life stained and debauched with sin. But God's *royal* intercessors come before Him with royal lives. Holy living promotes holy praying. God's intercessors "lift up holy hands," the symbols of righteous, obedient lives.

X

PRAYER AND OBEDIENCE (Continued)

"Many exemplary men have I known, holy in heart and life, within my four score years. But one equal to John Fletcher -- one so inwardly and outwardly obedient and devoted to God -- I have not known."

JOHN WESLEY

IT is worthy of note that the praying to which such transcendent position is given and from which great results are attributable, is not simply the saying of prayers, but holy praying. It is the "prayers of the saints," the prayers of the holy men of God. Behind such praying, giving to it energy and flame are the men and women who are wholly devoted to God, who are entirely separated from sin, and fully separated unto God. These are they who always give energy, force and strength to praying.

Our Lord Jesus Christ was preeminent in praying, because He was preeminent in saintliness. An entire dedication to God, a full surrender, which carries with it the whole being, in a flame of holy consecration -- all this gives wings to faith and energy to prayer. It opens the door to the throne of grace, and brings strong influence to bear on Almighty God.

The "lifting up of holy hands" is essential to Christly praying. It is not, however, a holiness which only dedicates a closet to God, which sets apart merely an hour to Him, but a consecration which takes hold of the entire man, which dedicates the whole life to God.

Our Lord Jesus Christ, "holy, harmless, undefiled, separate from sinners," had full liberty of approach and ready access to God in prayer. And He had this free and full access because of His unquestioning obedience to His Father. Right through His earthly life His supreme care and desire was to do the will of His Father.

And this fact, coupled with another -- the consciousness of having so ordered His life -- gave Him confidence and assurance, which enabled Him to draw near to the throne of grace with unbounded confidence, born of obedience, and promising acceptance, audience, and answer.

Loving obedience puts us where we can "ask anything in His name," with the assurance, that "He will do it." Loving obedience brings us into the prayer realm, and makes us beneficiaries of the wealth of Christ, and of the riches of His grace, through the coming of the Holy Spirit who will abide with us, and be in us. Cheerful obedience to God, qualifies us to pray effectually.

This obedience which not only qualifies but fore-runs prayer, must be loving, constant, always doing the Father's will, and cheerfully following the path of God's commands.

In the instance of King Hezekiah, it was a potent plea which changed God's decree that he should die and not live. The stricken ruler called upon God to remember how that he had walked before Him in truth, and with a perfect heart. With God, this counted. He hearkened to the petition, and, as a result, death found his approach to Hezekiah barred for fifteen years.

Jesus learned obedience in the school of suffering, and, at the same time, He learned prayer in the school of obedience. Just as it is the prayer of a righteous man which availeth much, so it is righteousness which is obedience to God. A righteous man is an obedient man, and he it is, who can pray effectually, who can accomplish great things when he betakes himself to his knees.

True praying, be it remembered, is not mere sentiment, nor poetry, nor eloquent utterance. Nor does it consist of saying in honeyed cadences, "Lord, Lord." Prayer is not a mere form of words; it is not just calling upon a Name. Prayer is obedience. It is founded on the adamantine rock of obedience to God. Only those who obey have the right to pray. Behind the praying must be the doing; and it is the constant doing of God's will in daily life which gives prayer its potency, as our Lord plainly taught:

> *"Not every one which saith unto Me,*
> *Lord, Lord, shall enter into the kingdom*

of heaven, but he that doeth the will of My Father which is in heaven. Many will say unto Me in that day, Lord, have we not prophesied in Thy Name, and in Thy Name have cast out devils? And in Thy Name done many wonderful works? And then will I profess unto them, I never knew you; depart from Me, ye that worketh iniquity."

No name, however precious and powerful, can protect and give efficiency to prayer which is unaccompanied by the doing of God's will. Neither can the doing, without the praying, protect from Divine disapproval. If the will of God does not master the life, the praying will be nothing but sickly sentiment. If prayer do not inspire, sanctify and direct our work, then self-will enters, to ruin both work and worker.

How great and manifold are the misconceptions of the true elements and functionings of prayer! There are many who earnestly desire to obtain an answer to their prayers but who go unrewarded and unblest. They fix their minds on some promise of God and then endeavour by dint of dogged perseverance, to summon faith sufficient to lay hold upon, and claim it. This fixing of the mind on some great promise may avail in *strengthening* faith, but, to this holding on to the promise must be added the persistent and importunate prayer that expects, and waits till faith grows exceedingly. And who is there that is able and competent to do such praying save the man who readily, cheerfully and continually, *obeys God?*

Faith, in its highest form, is the attitude as well as the act of a soul surrendered to God, in whom His Word and His Spirit dwells. It is true that faith must exist in some form, or another, in order to prompt praying; but in its strongest form, and in its largest results, faith is the fruit of prayer. That faith increases the ability and the efficiency of prayer is true; but it is likewise true that prayer increases the ability and efficiency of faith. Prayer and faith, work, act and react, one upon the other.

Obedience to God helps faith as no other attribute possibly can. When obedience -- implicit recognition of the validity, the paramountcy of the Divine commands -- faith ceases to be an almost superhuman task. It requires no straining to exercise it. Obedience to God makes it easy to believe and trust God. Where the spirit of obedience fully impregnates the soul; where the will is perfectly surrendered to God; where there is a fixed, unalterable purpose to obey God, faith almost believes itself. Faith then becomes almost involuntary. After obedience it is, naturally, the next step, and it is easily and readily taken. The difficulty in prayer is not with faith, but with obedience, which is faith's foundation.

We must look well to our obedience, to the secret springs of action, to the loyalty of our heart to God, if we would pray well, and desire to get the most out of our praying. Obedience is the groundwork of effectual praying; this it is, which brings us nigh to God.

The lack of obedience in our lives breaks down our praying. Quite often, the life is in revolt and this places us where praying is almost impossible, except it be for pardoning mercy. Disobedient living produces mighty poor praying. Disobedience shuts the door of the inner chamber, and bars the way to the Holy of holies. No man can pray -- really pray -- who does not obey.

The will must be surrendered to God as a primary condition of all successful praying. Everything about us gets its colouring from our inmost character. The secret will makes character and controls conduct. The will, therefore, plays an important part in all successful praying. There can be no praying in its richest implication and truest sense, where the will is not wholly and fully surrendered to God. This unswerving loyalty to God is an utterly indispensable condition of the best, the truest, the most effectual praying. We have "simply *got* to trust and obey; *there's no other way,* to be happy in Jesus -- but to trust, and *obey!* "

XI

PRAYER AND VIGILANCE

"David Brainerd was pursued by unearthly adversaries, who were resolved to rob him of his guerdon. He knew he must never quit his armour, but lie down to rest, with his corselet laced. The stains that marred the perfection of his lustrous dress, the spots of rust on his gleaming shield, are imperceptible to us; but they were, to him, the source of much sorrow and ardency of yearning."

LIFE OF DAVID BRAINERD

THE description of the Christian soldier given by Paul in the sixth chapter of the *Epistle to the Ephesians*, is compact and comprehensive. He is depicted as being ever in the conflict, which has many fluctuating seasons -- seasons of prosperity and adversity, light and darkness, victory and defeat. He is to pray at all seasons, and with all prayer, this to be added to the armour in which he is to fare forth to battle. At all times, he is to have the full panoply of prayer. The Christian soldier, if he fight to win, must pray much. By this means, only, is he enabled to defeat his inveterate enemy, the devil, together with the Evil One's manifold emissaries. "Praying always, with all prayer," is the Divine direction given him. This covers all seasons, and embraces all manner of praying.

Christian soldiers, fighting the good fight of faith, have access to a place of retreat, to which they continually repair for prayer. "Praying always, with all prayer," is a clear statement of the imperative need of much praying, and of many kinds of praying, by him who, fighting the good fight of faith, would win out, in the end, over all his foes.

The Revised Version puts it this way:

> *"With all prayer and supplication,*
> *praying at all seasons in the Spirit, and*
> *watching thereunto in all perseverance*
> *and supplications, for all saints, and on*
> *my behalf, that utterance may be given*
> *unto me, in opening my mouth to make*
> *known with boldness the mystery of the*
> *Gospel, for which I am in bonds."*

It cannot be stated too frequently that the life of a Christian is a warfare, an intense conflict, a lifelong contest. It is a battle, moreover, waged against invisible foes, who are ever alert, and ever seeking to entrap, deceive, and ruin the souls of men. The life to which Holy Scripture calls men is no picnic, or holiday junketing. It is no pastime, no pleasure jaunt. It entails effort, wrestling, struggling; it demands the putting forth of the full energy of the spirit in order to frustrate the foe and to come off, at the last, more than conqueror. It is no primrose path, no rose-scented dalliance. From start to finish, it is war. From the hour in which he first draws sword, to that in which he doffs his harness, the Christian warrior is compelled to "endure hardness like a good soldier."

What a misconception many people have of the Christian life! How little the average church member appears to know of the character of the conflict, and of its demands upon him! How ignorant he seems to be of the enemies he must encounter, if he engage to serve God faithfully and so succeed in getting to heaven and receive the crown of life! He seems scarcely to realize that the world, the flesh and the devil will oppose his onward march, and will defeat him utterly, unless he give himself to constant vigilance and unceasing prayer.

The Christian soldier wrestles not against flesh and blood, but against spiritual wickedness in high places. Or, as the Scriptural margin reads, "wicked spirits in high places." What a fearful array of forces are set against him who would make his way through the wilderness of this world to the portals of the Celestial City! It is no surprise, therefore, to find Paul, who understood the character of the Christian life so well, and who was so thoroughly informed as to the malignity and number of the foes, which the disciple of the Lord must encounter, carefully and plainly urging him to "put on the whole armour of God," and "to pray with all prayer and supplication in the Spirit." Wise, with a great wisdom, would the present generation be if all professors of our faith could be induced to realize this all-important and vital truth, which is so absolutely indispensable to a successful Christian life.

It is just at this point in much present-day Christian profession, that one may find its greatest defect. There is little, or nothing, of the soldier element in it. The discipline, self-denial, spirit of hardship, determination, so prominent in and belonging to the military life, are, one and all, largely wanting. Yet the Christian life is *warfare*, all the way.

How comprehensive, pointed and striking are all Paul's directions to the Christian soldier, who is bent on thwarting the devil and saving his soul alive! First of all, he must possess a clear idea of the character of the life on which he has entered. Then, he must know something of his foes -- the adversaries of his immortal soul -- their strength, their skill, their malignity. Knowing, therefore, something of the character of the enemy, and realizing the need of preparation to overcome them, he is prepared to hear the Apostle's decisive conclusion:

> *"Finally, my brethren, be strong in the Lord, and in he power of His might. Put on the whole armour of God, that ye may be able to stand against the wiles of the devil. Wherefore, take unto you the whole armour of God, that ye may be able to stand in the evil day, and having done all, to stand."*

All these directions end in a climax; and that climax is prayer. How can the brave warrior for Christ be made braver still? How can the strong soldier be made stronger still? How can the victorious battler be made still more victorious? Here are Paul's explicit directions to that end:

*"Praying always with all prayer and
supplication in the Spirit, and watching
thereunto with all perseverance and
supplication for all saints."*

Prayer, and more prayer, adds to the fighting qualities and the more certain victories of God's good fighting-men. The power of prayer is most forceful on the battle-field amid the din and strife of the conflict. Paul was preeminently a soldier of the Cross. For him, life was no flowery bed of ease. He was no dress-parade, holiday soldier, whose only business was to don a uniform on set occasions. His was a life of intense conflict, the facing of many adversaries, the exercise of unsleeping vigilance and constant effort. And, at its close -- in sight of the end -- we hear him chanting his final song of victory, a I have fought a good fight," and reading between the lines, we see that he is more than conqueror!

In his *Epistle to the Romans,* Paul indicates the nature of his soldier-life, giving us some views of the kind of praying needed for such a career. He writes:

*"Now I beseech you, brethren, for the
Lord Jesus Christ's sake, and for the
love of the Spirit, that ye strive together
with me in your prayers to God for me,
that I may be delivered from them that
do not believe in Judaea."*

Paul *had* foes in Judaea -- foes who beset and opposed him in the form of "unbelieving men" and this, added to other weighty reasons, led him to urge the Roman Christians to "strive with him in prayer." That word "strive" indicated wrestling, the putting forth of great effort. This is the kind of effort, and this the sort of spirit, which must possess the Christian soldier.

Here is a great soldier, a captain-general, in the great struggle, faced by malignant forces who seek his ruin. His force is well-nigh spent. What reinforcements can he count on? What can give help and bring success to a warrior in such a pressing emergency? It is a critical moment in the conflict. What force can be added to the energy of his own prayers? The answer is -- in the prayers of others, even the prayers of his brethren who were at Rome. These, he believes, will bring him additional aid, so that he can win his fight, overcome his adversaries, and, ultimately, prevail.

The Christian soldier is to pray at all seasons, and under all circumstances. His praying must be arranged so as to cover his times of peace as well as his hours of active conflict. It must be available in his marching and his fighting. Prayer must diffuse all effort, impregnate all ventures, decide all issues. The Christian soldier must be as intense in his praying as in his fighting, for his victories will depend very much more on his praying than on his fighting. Fervent supplication must be added to steady resolve, prayer and supplication must supplement the armour of God. The Holy Spirit must aid the supplication with His own strenuous plea. And the soldier must pray in the Spirit. In this, as in other forms of warfare, eternal vigilance is the price of victory; and thus, watchfulness and persistent perseverance, must mark the every activity of the Christian warrior.

The soldier-prayer must reflect its profound concern for the success and well-being of the whole army. The battle is not altogether a personal matter; victory cannot be achieved for self, alone. There is a sense, in which the entire army of Christ is involved. The cause of God, His saints, their woes and trials, their duties and crosses, all should find a voice and a pleader in the Christian soldier, when he prays. He dare not limit his praying to himself. Nothing dries up spiritual secretions so certainly and completely; nothing poisons the fountain of spiritual life so effectively; nothing acts in such deadly fashion, as selfish praying.

Note carefully that the Christian's armour will avail him nothing, unless prayer be added. This is the pivot, the connecting link of the armour of God. This holds it together, and renders it effective. God's true soldier plans his campaigns, arranges his battle-forces, and conducts his conflicts, with prayer. It is all important and absolutely essential to victory, that prayer should so impregnate the life that every breath will be a petition, every sigh a supplication. The Christian soldier must needs be always fighting. He should, of sheer necessity, be always praying.

The Christian soldier is compelled to constant picket-duty. He must always be on his guard. He is faced by a foe who never sleeps, who is always alert, and ever prepared to take advantage of the fortunes of war. Watchfulness is a cardinal principle with Christ's warrior, "watch and pray," forever sounding in his ears. He cannot dare to be asleep at his post. Such a lapse brings him not only under the displeasure of the Captain of his salvation, but exposes him to added danger. Watchfulness, therefore, imperatively constitutes the duty of the soldier of the Lord.

In the New Testament, there are three different words, which are translated "watch." The first means "absence of sleep," and implies a wakeful frame of mind, as opposed to listlessness; it is an enjoinder to keep awake, circumspect, attentive, constant, vigilant. The second word means "fully awake," -- a state induced by some rousing effort, which faculty excited to attention and interest, active, cautious, lest through carelessness or indolence, some destructive calamity should suddenly evolve. The third word means "to be calm and collected in spirit," dispassionate, untouched by slumberous or beclouding influences, a wariness against all pitfalls and beguilements.

All three definitions are used by St. Paul. Two of them are employed in connection with prayer. Watchfulness intensified, is a requisite for prayer. Watchfulness must guard and cover the whole spiritual man, and fit him for prayer. Everything resembling unpreparedness or non-vigilance, is death to prayer.

In *Ephesians*, Paul gives prominence to the duty of constant watchfulness, "Watching thereunto with all perseverance and supplication." Watch, he says, *watch*, WATCH! "And what I say unto you, I say unto all, Watch."

Sleepless wakefulness is the price one must pay for victory over his spiritual foes. Rest assured that the devil never falls asleep. He is ever "walking about, seeking whom he may devour." Just as a shepherd must never be careless and unwatchful lest the wolf devour his sheep, so the Christian soldier must ever have his eyes wide open, implying his possession of a spirit which neither slumbers nor grows careless. The inseparable companions and safeguards of prayer are vigilance, watchfulness, and a mounted guard. In writing to the Colossians Paul brackets these inseparable qualities together: "Continue in prayer," he enjoins, "and watch in the same, with thanksgiving."

When will Christians more thoroughly learn the twofold lesson, that they are called to a great warfare, and that in order to get the victory they must give themselves to unsleeping watchfulness and unceasing prayer?

> *"Be sober, be vigilant," says Peter,*
> *"because your adversary, the devil,*
> *walketh about seeking whom he may*
> *devour."*

God's Church is a militant host. Its warfare is with unseen forces of evil. God's people compose an army fighting to establish His kingdom in the earth. Their aim is to destroy the sovereignty of Satan, and over its ruins, erect the Kingdom of God, which is "righteousness and peace and joy in the Holy Ghost." This militant army is composed of individual soldiers of the Cross, and the armour of God is needed for its defence. Prayer must be added as that which crowns the whole.

> *"Stand then in His great might, With*
> *all His strength endued; But take, to*
> *arm you for the fight, The panoply of*
> *God."*

Prayer is too simple, too evident a duty, to need definition. Necessity gives being and shape to prayer. Its importance is so absolute, that the Christian soldier's life, in all the breadth and intensity of it, should be one of prayer. The entire life of a Christian soldier -- its being, intention, implication and action -- are all dependent on its being a life of prayer. Without prayer -- no matter what else he have -- the Christian soldier's life will be feeble, and ineffective, and constitute him an easy prey for his spiritual enemies.

Christian experience will be sapless, and Christian influence will be dry and arid, unless prayer has a high place in the life. Without prayer the Christian graces will wither and die. Without prayer, we may add, preaching is edgeless and a vain thing, and the Gospel loses its wings and its loins. Christ is the lawgiver of prayer, and Paul is His Apostle of prayer. Both declare its primacy and importance, and demonstrate the fact of its indispensability. Their prayer-directions cover all places, include all times, and comprehend all things. How, then, can the Christian soldier hope or dream of victory, unless he be fortified by its power? How can he fail, if in addition to putting on the armour of God he be, at all times and seasons, "watching unto prayer"?

XII

PRAYER AND THE WORD OF GOD

"How constantly, in the Scriptures, do we encounter such words as 'field,' 'seed,' 'sower,' 'reaper,' 'seed-time,' 'harvest'! Employing such metaphors interprets a fact of nature by a parable of grace. The field is the world and the good seed is the Word of God .Whether the Word be spoken or written, it is the power of God unto salvation. In our work of evangelism, the whole world is our field, every creature the object of effort and every book and tract, a seed of God."

DAVID FANT, JR.

GOD'S Word is a record of prayer -- of praying men and their achievements, of the Divine warrant of prayer and of the encouragement given to those who pray. No one can read the instances, commands, examples, multiform statements which concern themselves with prayer, without realizing that the cause of God, and the success of His work in this world is committed to prayer; that praying men have been God's vicegerents on earth; that prayerless men have never been used of Him.

A reverence for God's holy Name is closely related to a high regard for His Word. This hallowing of God's Name; the ability to do His will on earth, as it is done in heaven; the establishment and glory of God's kingdom, are as much involved in prayer, as when Jesus taught men the Universal Prayer. That "men ought always to pray and not to faint," is as fundamental to God's cause, today, as when Jesus Christ enshrined that great truth in the immortal settings of the Parable of the Importunate Widow.

As God's house is called "the house of prayer," because prayer is the most important of its holy offices; so by the same token, the

Bible may be called the Book of Prayer. Prayer is the great theme and content of its message to mankind.

God's Word is the basis, as it is the directory of the prayer of faith. "Let the word of Christ dwell in you richly in all wisdom," says St. Paul, "teaching and admonishing one another in psalms and hymns and spiritual songs, singing with grace in your hearts to the Lord."

As this word of Christ dwelling in us richly is transmuted and assimilated, it issues in praying. Faith is constructed of the Word and the Spirit, and faith is the body and substance of prayer.

In many of its aspects, prayer is dependent upon the Word of God. Jesus says:

*"If ye abide in Me, and My words abide
in you, ye shall ask what ye will, and it
shall be done unto you."*

The Word of God is the fulcrum upon which the lever of prayer is placed, and by which things are mightily moved. God has committed Himself, His purpose and His promise to prayer. His Word becomes the basis, the inspiration of our praying, and there are circumstances under which, by importunate prayer, we may obtain an addition, or an enlargement of His promises. It is said of the old saints that they, "through faith obtained promises." There would seem to be in prayer the capacity for going even beyond the Word, of getting even beyond His promise, into the very presence of God, Himself.

Jacob wrestled, not so much with a promise, as with the Promiser. We must take hold of the Promiser, lest the promise prove nugatory. Prayer may well be defined as that force which vitalizes and energizes the Word of God, by taking hold of God, Himself. By taking hold of the Promiser, prayer reissues, and makes personal the promise. "There is none that stirreth up himself to take hold of Me," is God's sad lament. "Let him take hold of My strength, that he may make peace with Me," is God's recipe for prayer.

By Scriptural warrant, prayer may be divided into the petition of faith and that of submission. The prayer of faith is based on the written Word, for "faith cometh by hearing, and hearing by the Word of God." It receives its answer, inevitably -- the very thing for which it prays.

The prayer of submission is without a definite word of promise, so to speak, but takes hold of God with a lowly and contrite spirit, and asks and pleads with Him, for that which the soul desires. Abraham had no definite promise that God would spare Sodom. Moses had no definite promise that God would spare Israel; on the contrary, there was the declaration of His wrath, and of His purpose to destroy. But the devoted leader gained his plea with God, when he interceded for the Israelites with incessant prayers and many tears. Daniel had no definite promise that God would reveal to him the meaning of the king's dream, but he prayed specifically, and God answered definitely.

The Word of God is made effectual and operative, by the process and practice of prayer. The Word of the Lord came to Elijah, "Go show thyself to Ahab, and I will send rain on the earth." Elijah showed himself to Ahab; but the answer to his prayer did not come, until he had pressed his fiery prayer upon the Lord seven times.

Paul had the definite promise from Christ, that he "would be delivered from the people and the Gentiles," but we find him exhorting the Romans in the urgent and solemn manner concerning this very matter:

"Now I beseech you, brethren, for the Lord Jesus Christ's sake, and for the love of the Spirit, that ye strive together with me in your prayers to God for me; that I may be delivered from them that do not believe in Judaea, and that my service which I have for Jerusalem may be accepted of the saints."

The Word of God is a great help in prayer. If it be lodged and written in our hearts, it will form an outflowing current of prayer, full and irresistible. Promises, stored in the heart, are to be the fuel from which prayer receives life and warmth, just as the coal, stored in the earth, ministers to our comfort on stormy days and wintry nights. The Word of God is the food, by which prayer is nourished and made strong. Prayer, like man, cannot live by bread alone, "but by every word which proceedeth out of the mouth of the Lord."

Unless the vital forces of prayer are supplied by God's Word, prayer, though earnest, even vociferous, in its urgency, is, in reality, flabby, and vapid, and void. The absence of vital force in praying, can be traced to the absence of a constant supply of God's Word, to repair the waste, and renew the life. He who would learn to pray well, must first study God's Word, and store it in his memory and thought.

When we consult God's Word, we find that no duty is more binding, more exacting, than that of prayer. On the other hand, we discover that no privilege is more exalted, no habit more richly owned of God. No promises are more radiant, more abounding, more explicit, more often reiterated, than those which are attached to prayer. "All things, whatsoever" are received by prayer, because "all things whatsoever" are promised. There is no limit to the provisions, included in the promises to prayer, and no exclusion from its promises. "Every one that asketh, receiveth." The word of our Lord is to this all-embracing effect: "If ye shall ask anything in My Name, I will do it."

Here are some of the comprehensive, and exhaustive statements of the Word of God about prayer, the things to be taken in by prayer, the strong promise made in answer to prayer:

> *"Pray without ceasing;" "continue in prayer;" "continuing instant in prayer;" "in everything by prayer, let your request be made known unto God;" "pray always, pray and not faint;" "men should pray everywhere;" "praying always, with all prayer and supplication."*

What clear and strong statements are those which are put in the Divine record, to furnish us with a sure basis of faith, and to urge, constrain and encourage us to pray! How wide the range of prayer, as given us, in the Divine Revelation! How these Scriptures incite us to seek the God of prayer, with all our wants, with all our burdens!

In addition to these statements left on record for our encouragement, the sacred pages teem with facts, examples, incidents, and observations, stressing the importance and the absolute necessity of prayer, and putting emphasis on its all-prevailing power.

The utmost reach and full benefit of the rich promises of the Word of God, should humbly be received by us, and put to the test. The world will never receive the full benefits of the Gospel until this be done. Neither Christian experience nor Christian living will be what they ought to be till these Divine promises have been fully tested by those who pray. By prayer, we bring these promises of God's holy will into the realm of the actual and the real. Prayer is the philosopher's stone which transmutes them into gold.

If it be asked, what is to be done in order to render God's promises real, the answer is, that we must pray, until the words of the promise are clothed upon with the rich raiment of fulfilment.

God's promises are altogether too large to be mastered by desultory praying. When we examine ourselves, all too often, we discover that our praying does not rise to the demands of the situation; is so limited that it is little more than a mere oasis amid the waste and desert of the world's sin. Who of us, in our praying, measures up to this promise of our Lord:

> *"Verily, verily, I say unto you, He that believeth on Me, the works that I do shall he do also, and greater works than these shall he do, because I go to My Father."*

How comprehensive, how far reaching, how all-embracing! How much is here, for the glory of God, how much for the good of man! How much for the manifestation of Christ's enthroned power, how much for the reward of abundant faith! And how great and gracious are the results which can be made to accrue from the exercise of commensurate, believing prayer!

Look, for a moment, at another of God's great promises, and discover how we may be undergirded by the Word as we pray, and on what firm ground we may stand on which to make our petitions to our God:

> *"If ye abide in Me, and My words abide*
> *in you, ye shall ask what ye will, and it*
> *shall be done unto you."*

In these comprehensive words, God turns Himself over to the will of His people. When Christ becomes our all-in-all, prayer lays God's treasures at our feet. Primitive Christianity had an easy and practical solution of the situation, and got all which God had to give. That simple and terse solution is recorded in John's *First Epistle:*

> *"Whatsoever we ask, we receive of Him,*
> *because we keep His commandments,*
> *and do those things which are pleasing*
> *in His sight."*

Prayer, coupled with loving obedience, is the way to put God to the test, and to make prayer answer all ends and all things. Prayer, joined to the Word of God, hallows and makes sacred all God's gifts. Prayer is not simply to get things from God, but to make those things holy, which already have been received from Him. It is not merely to get a blessing, but also to be able to give a blessing. Prayer makes common things holy and secular things, sacred. It receives things from God with thanksgiving and hallows them with thankful hearts, and devoted service.

In the *First Epistle to Timothy*, Paul gives us these words:

> *"For every creature of God is good, and*
> *nothing to be refused, if it be received*
> *with thanksgiving. For it is sanctified*
> *by the word of God and prayer."*

That is a statement which gives a negative to mere asceticism. God's good gifts are to be holy, not only by God's creative power, but, also, because they are made holy to us by prayer. We receive them, appropriate them and sanctify them by prayer.

Doing God's will, and having His Word abiding in us, is an imperative of effectual praying. But, it may be asked, how are we to know what God's will is? The answer is, by studying His Word, by hiding it in our hearts, and by letting the Word dwell in us richly. "The entrance of Thy word, giveth light."

To know God's will in prayer, we must be filled with God's Spirit, who maketh intercession for the saints, and in the saints, according to the will of God. To be filled with God's Spirit, to be filled with God's Word, is to know God's will. It is to be put in such a frame of mind, to be found in such a state of heart, as will enable us to read and interpret aright the purposes of the Infinite. Such filling of the heart, with the Word and the Spirit, gives us an insight into the will of the Father, and enables us to rightly discern His will, and puts within us, a disposition of mind and heart to make it the guide and compass of our lives.

Epaphras prayed that the Colossians might stand "perfect and complete in all the will of God." This is proof positive that, not only may we know the will of God, but that we may know *all* the will of God. And not only may we know all the will of God, but we may *do* all the will of God. We may, moreover, do all the will of God, not occasionally, or by a mere impulse, but with a settled habit of conduct. Still further, it shows us that we may not only do the will of God externally, but from the heart, doing it cheerfully, without reluctance, or secret disinclination, or any drawing or holding back from the intimate presence of the Lord.

XIII

PRAYER AND THE WORD OF GOD (Continued)

"Some years ago a man was travelling in the wilds of Kentucky. He had with him a large sum of money and was well armed. He put up at a log-house one night, but was much concerned with the rough appearance of the men who came and went from this abode. He retired early but not to sleep. At midnight he heard the dogs barking furiously and the sound of someone entering the cabin. Peering through a chink in the boards of his room, he saw a stranger with a gun in his hand. Another man sat before the fire. The traveller concluded they were planning to rob him, and prepared to defend himself and his property. Presently the newcomer took down a copy of the Bible, read a chapter aloud, and then knelt down and prayed. The traveller dismissed his fears, put his revolver away and lay down, to sleep peacefully until morning light. And all because a Bible was in the cabin, and its owner a man of prayer."

REV. F. F. SHOUP.

PRAYER has all to do with the success of the preaching of the Word. This, Paul clearly teaches in that familiar and pressing request he made to the Thessalonians:

> *"Finally, brethren, pray for us that the*
> *Word of the Lord may have free course,*
> *and be glorified."*

Prayer opens the way for the Word of God to run without let or hindrance, and creates the atmosphere which is favourable to the word accomplishing its purpose. Prayer puts wheels under God's Word, and gives wings to the angel of the Lord "having the everlasting Gospel to preach unto them that dwell on the earth, and to every nation, and kindred, and tongue, and people." Prayer greatly helps the Word of the Lord.

The Parable of the Sower is a notable study of preaching, showing its differing effects and describing the diversity of hearers. The wayside hearers are legion. The soil lies all unprepared either by previous thought or prayer; as a consequence, the devil easily takes away the seed (which is the Word of God) and dissipating all good impressions, renders the work of the sower futile. No one for a moment believes, that so much of present-day sowing would go fruitless if only the hearers would prepare the ground of their hearts beforehand by prayer and meditation.

Similarly with the stony-ground hearers, and the thorny-ground hearers. Although the word lodges in their hearts and begins to sprout, yet all is lost, chiefly because there is no prayer or watchfulness or cultivation following. The good-ground hearers are profited by the sowing, simply because their minds have been prepared for the reception of the seed, and that, after hearing, they have cultivated the seed sown in their hearts, by the exercise of prayer. All this gives peculiar emphasis to the conclusion of this striking parable: "Take heed, therefore, how ye hear." And in order that *we* may take heed how we hear, it is needful to give ourselves continually to prayer.

We have *got* to believe that underlying God's Word is prayer, and upon prayer, its final success will depend. In the *Book of Isaiah* we read:

> *"So shall My word be that goeth out of My mouth; it shall not return unto Me void, but it shall accomplish that which I please, and it shall prosper in the thing whereto I sent it."*

In Psalm 19, David magnifies the Word of God in six statements concerning it. It converts the soul, makes wise the simple, rejoices the heart, enlightens the eyes, endures eternally, and is true and righteous altogether. The Word of God is perfect, sure, right, pure. It is heart-searching, and at the same time purifying, in its effect. It is no surprise therefore that after considering the deep spirituality of the Word of God, its power to search the inner nature of man, and its deep purity, the Psalmist should close his dissertation with this passage:

> *"Who can understand his errors?" And then praying after this fashion: "Cleanse Thou me from secret faults. Keep back Thy servant also from presumptuous sins. Let them not have dominion over me. Let the words of my mouth, and the meditations of my heart be acceptable in Thy sight, O Lord, my strength and my redeemer."*

James recognizes the deep spirituality of the Word, and its inherent saving power, in the following exhortation:

> *"Wherefore, lay apart all filthiness and superfluity of naughtiness, and receive with meekness the engrafted word, which is able to save your souls."*

And Peter talks along the same line, when describing the saving power of the Word of God:

> *"Being born again, not of corruptible seed, but of incorruptible, by the word of God, which liveth and abideth forever."*

Not only does Peter speak of being born again, by the incorruptible Word of God, but he informs us that to grow in grace we must be like new-born babes, desiring or feeding upon the "sincere milk of the Word."

That is not to say, however, that the mere form of words as they occur in the Bible have in them any saving efficacy. But the Word of God, be it remembered, is impregnated with the Holy

Spirit. And just as there is a Divine element in the words of Scripture, so also is the same Divine element to be found in all true preaching of the Word, which is able to save and convert the soul.

Prayer invariably begets a love for the Word of God, and sets people to the reading of it. Prayer leads people to obey the Word of God, and puts into the heart which obeys a joy unspeakable. Praying people and Bible-reading people are the same sort of folk. The God of the Bible and the God of prayer are one. God speaks to man in the Bible; man speaks to God in prayer. One reads the Bible to discover God's will; he prays in order that he may receive power to do that will. Bible-reading and praying are the distinguishing traits of those who strive to know and please God. And just as prayer begets a love for the Scriptures, and sets people to reading the Bible, so, also, does prayer cause men and women to visit the house of God, to hear the Scriptures expounded. Church-going is closely connected with the Bible, not so much because the Bible cautions us against "forsaking the assembling of ourselves together as the manner of some is," but because in God's house, God's chosen minister declares His Word to dying men, explains the Scriptures, and enforces their teachings upon his hearers. And prayer germinates a resolve, in those who practise it, not to forsake the house of God.

Prayer begets a church-going conscience, a church-loving heart, a church-supporting spirit. It is the praying people, who make it a matter of conscience, to attend the preaching of the Word; who delight in its reading; exposition; who support it with their influence and their means. Prayer exalts the Word of God and gives it preeminence in the estimation of those who faithfully and wholeheartedly call upon the Name of the Lord.

Prayer draws its very life from the Bible, and has no standing ground outside of the warrant of the Scriptures. Its very existence and character is dependent on revelation made by God to man in His holy Word. Prayer, in turn, exalts this same revelation, and turns men toward that Word. The nature, necessity and all-comprehending character of prayer, is based on the Word of God.

Psalm 119 is a directory of God's Word. With three or four exceptions, each verse contains a word which identifies, or locates, the Word of God. Quite often, the writer breaks out into supplication, several times praying, "Teach me Thy statutes." So deeply impressed is he with the wonders of God's Word, and of the need for Divine illumination wherewith to see and understand the wonderful things recorded therein, that he fervently prays:

> *"Open Thou mine eyes, that I may behold wondrous things out of Thy law."*

From the opening of this wonderful Psalm to its close, prayer and God's Word are intertwined. Almost every phase of God's Word is touched upon by this inspired writer. So thoroughly convinced was the Psalmist of the deep spiritual power of the Word of God that he makes this declaration:

> *"Thy word have I hid in my heart that I might not sin against Thee."*

Here the Psalmist found his protection against sinning. By having God's Word hidden in his heart; in having his whole being thoroughly impregnated with that Word; in being brought completely under its benign and gracious influence, he was enabled to walk to and fro in the earth, safe from the attack of the Evil One, and fortified against a proneness to wander out of the way.

We find, furthermore, the power of prayer to create a real love for the Scriptures, and to put within men a nature which will take pleasure in the Word. In holy ecstasy he cries, "O, how I love Thy law! It is my meditation all the day." And again: "How sweet are Thy words to my taste! Yea, sweeter than honey to my taste."

Would we have a relish for God's Word? Then let us give ourselves continually to prayer. He who would have a heart for the reading of the Bible must not -- dare not -- forget to pray. The man of whom it can be said, "His delight is in the law of the Lord," is the man who can truly say, "I delight to visit the place of prayer." No man loves the Bible, who does not love to pray. No man loves to pray, who does not delight in the law of the Lord.

Our Lord was a man of prayer, and He magnified the Word of God, quoting often from the Scriptures. Right through His earthly life Jesus observed Sabbath-keeping, church-going and the reading of the Word of God, and had prayer intermingled with them all:

> *"And He came to Nazareth where He*
> *had been brought up, and as His custom*
> *was, He went into the synagogue on the*
> *Sabbath Day, and stood up to read."*

Here, let it be said, that no two things are more essential to a spirit-filled life than Bible-reading and secret prayer; no two things more helpful to growth in grace; to getting the largest joy out of a Christian life; toward establishing one in the ways of eternal peace. The neglect of these all-important duties, presages leanness of soul, loss of joy, absence of peace, dryness of spirit, decay in all that pertains to spiritual life. Neglecting these things paves the way for apostasy, and gives the Evil One an advantage such as he is not likely to ignore. Reading God's Word regularly, and praying habitually in the secret place of the Most High puts one where he is absolutely safe from the attacks of the enemy of souls, and guarantees him salvation and final victory, through the overcoming power of the Lamb.

XIV

PRAYER AND THE HOUSE OF GOD

"And dear to me the loud 'Amen,' Which echoes through the blest abode -- Which swells, and sinks, then swells again, Dies on the walls -- but lives with God! "

PRAYER stands related to places, times, occasions and circumstances. It has to do with God and with everything which is related to God, and it has an intimate and special relationship to His house. A church is a sacred place, set apart from all unhallowed and secular uses, for the worship of God. As worship is prayer, the house of God is a place set apart for worship. It is no common place; it is where God dwells, where He meets with His people, and He delights in the worship of His saints.

Prayer is always in place in the house of God. When prayer is a stranger there, then it ceases to be God's house at all. Our Lord put peculiar emphasis upon what the Church was when He cast out the buyers and sellers in the Temple, repeating the words from Isaiah, "It is written, My house shall be called the house of prayer." He makes prayer preeminent, that which stands out above all else in the house of God. They, who sidetrack prayer or seek to minify it, and give it a secondary place, pervert the Church of God, and make it something less and other than it is ordained to be.

Prayer is perfectly at home in the house of God. It is no stranger, no mere guest; it belongs there. It has a peculiar affinity for the place, and has, moreover, a Divine right there, being set, therein, by Divine appointment and approval.

The inner chamber is a sacred place for personal worship. The house of God is a holy place for united worship. The prayer-closet is for individual prayer. The house of God is for mutual prayer, concerted prayer, united prayer. Yet even in the house of God, there is the element of private worship, since God's people are to worship

Him and pray to Him, personally, even in public worship. The Church is for the united prayer of kindred, yet individual believers.

The life, power and glory of the Church is prayer. The life of its members is dependent on prayer and the presence of God is secured and retained by prayer. The very place is made sacred by its ministry. Without it, the Church is lifeless and powerless. Without it, even the building, itself, is nothing, more or other, than any other structure. Prayer converts even the bricks, and mortar, and lumber, into a sanctuary, a holy of holies, where the Shekinah dwells. It separates it, in spirit and in purpose from all other edifices. Prayer gives a peculiar sacredness to the building, sanctifies it, sets it apart for God, conserves it from all common and mundane affairs.

With prayer, though the house of God might be supposed to lack everything else, it becomes a Divine sanctuary. So the Tabernacle, moving about from place to place, became the holy of holies, because prayer was there. Without prayer the building may be costly, perfect in all its appointments, beautiful for situation and attractive to the eye, but it comes down to the human, with nothing Divine in it, and is on a level with all other buildings.

Without prayer, a church is like a body without spirit; it is a dead, inanimate thing. A church with prayer in it, has God in it. When prayer is set aside, God is outlawed. When prayer becomes an unfamiliar exercise, then God Himself is a stranger there.

As God's house is a house of prayer, the Divine intention is that people should leave their homes and go to meet Him in His own house. The building is set apart for prayer especially, and as God has made special promise to meet His people there, it is their duty to go there, and for that specific end. Prayer should be the chief attraction for all spiritually minded church-goers. While it is conceded that the preaching of the Word has an important place in the house of God, yet prayer is its predominating, distinguishing feature. Not that all other places are sinful, or evil, in themselves or in their uses. But they are secular and human, having no special conception of God in them. The Church is, essentially, religious and

Divine. The work belonging to other places is done without special reference to God. He is not specifically recognized, nor called upon. In the Church, however, God is acknowledged, and nothing is done without Him. Prayer is the one distinguishing mark of the house of God. As prayer distinguishes Christian from unchristian people, so prayer distinguishes God's house from all other houses. It is a place where faithful believers meet with their Lord.

As God's house is, preeminently, a house of prayer, prayer should enter into and underlie everything that is undertaken there. Prayer be longs to every sort of work appertaining to the Church of God. As God's house is a house where the business of praying is carried on, so is it a place where the business of making praying people out of prayerless people is done. The house of God is a Divine workshop, and there the work of prayer goes on. Or the house of God is a Divine schoolhouse, in which the lesson of prayer is taught; where men and women learn to pray, and where they are graduated, in the school of prayer.

Any church calling itself the house of God, and failing to magnify prayer; which does not put prayer in the forefront of its activities; which does not teach the great lesson of prayer, should change its teaching to conform to the Divine pattern or change the name of its building to something other than a house of prayer.

On an earlier page, we made reference to the finding of the Book of the Law of the Lord given to Moses. How long that book had been there, we do not know. But when tidings of its discovery were carried to Josiah, he rent his clothes and was greatly disturbed. He lamented the neglect of God's Word and saw, as a natural result, the iniquity which abounded throughout the land.

And then, Josiah thought of God, and commanded Hilkiah, the priest, to go and make inquiry of the Lord. Such neglect of the Word of the Law was too serious a matter to be treated lightly, and God must be enquired of, and repentance shown, by himself, and the nation:

"Go enquire of the Lord for me, and for
them that are left in Israel and in Judah,

concerning the words of the book that is
found; for great is the wrath of the Lord
that is poured out upon us, because our
fathers have not kept the word of the
Lord, to do after all that is written in
this book."

But that was not all. Josiah was bent on promoting a revival of religion in his kingdom, so we find him gathering all the elders of Jerusalem and Judah together, for that purpose. When they had come together, the king went into the house of the Lord, and himself read in all the words of the Book of the Covenant that was found in the house of the Lord.

With this righteous king, God's Word was of great importance. He esteemed it at its proper worth, and counted a knowledge of it to be of such grave importance, as to demand his consulting God in prayer about it, and to warrant the gathering together of the notables of his kingdom, so that they, together with himself, should be instructed out of God's Book concerning God's Law.

When Ezra, returned from Babylon, was seeking the reconstruction of his nation, the people, themselves, were alive to the situation, and, on one occasion, the priests, Levites and people assembled themselves together as one man before the water gate.

"And they spake unto Ezra the scribe, to
bring the book of the law of Moses,
which the Lord had commanded to
Israel. And Ezra the priest brought the
law before the congregation, both of men
and women, and all that could hear with
understanding. And he read therein
before the street that was before the
water gate from the morning until
midday; and the ears of all the people
were attentive unto the book of the law."

This was Bible-reading Day in Judah -- a real revival of Scripture-study. The leaders read the law before the people, whose ears were keen to hear what God had to say to them out of the Book of the Law. But it was not only a Bible-reading day. It was a time when real preaching was done, as the following passage indicates:

"So they read in the book in the law of God distinctly and gave the sense, and caused them to understand the reading."

Here then is the Scriptural definition of preaching. No better definition can be given. To read the Word of God distinctly -- to read it so that the people could hear and understand the words read; not to mumble out the words, nor read it in an undertone or with indistinctness, but boldly and clearly -- that was the method followed in Jerusalem, on this auspicious day. Moreover: the sense of the words was made clear in the meeting held before the water gate; the people were treated to a high type of expository preaching. That was *true* preaching -- preaching of a sort which is sorely needed, today, in order that God's Word may have due effect on the hearts of the people. This meeting in Jerusalem surely contains a lesson which all present-day preachers should learn and heed.

No one having any knowledge of the existing facts, will deny the comparative lack of expository preaching in the pulpit effort of today. And none, we should, at least, imagine, will do other than lament the lack. Topical preaching, polemical preaching, historical preaching, and other forms of sermonic output have, one supposes, their rightful and opportune uses. But expository preaching -- the prayerful expounding of the Word of God is preaching that *is* preaching -- pulpit effort *par excellence*.

For its successful accomplishment, however, a preacher needs must be a man of prayer. For every hour spent in his study-chair, he will have to spend two upon his knees. For every hour he devotes to wrestling with an obscure passage of Holy Writ, he must have two in the which to be found wrestling with God. Prayer and preaching: preaching and prayer! They cannot be separated. The ancient cry was: "To your tents, O Israel! "The modern cry should be: "To your knees, O preachers, to your knees!"

Printed in the United States
99568LV00005B/79-81/A